SENIOR HIGH VOL. 5

Pacesetter

The Complete Youth Ministry Resource

Life Choices

TACKLING THE BIGGEST DECISIONS YOU'LL MAKE

■

David C. Cook Publishing Co.

Elgin, Illinois/Weston, Ontario

Senior High PACESETTER

■

LIFE CHOICES
Tackling the Biggest Decisions You'll Make

DAVID C. COOK PUBLISHING CO.
Elgin, Illinois/Weston, Ontario
LIFE CHOICES
Tackling the Biggest Decisions
You'll Make
© 1986 David C. Cook Publishing
Co.
All rights reserved. Except where
noted otherwise in the text, no
part of this publication may be re-
produced without permission of
the publisher.

■

Creative Team

Project Editor: Kevin A. Miller
Editors: Anne E. Dinnan; Paul N.
Woods
Assistant Editor: Eric Potter
Designer: Jill E. Novak

■

Management Team

David C. Cook III, Editor in Chief
Joseph Bayly, President
Ralph Gates, Director of Church
Resources
Marlene D. LeFever, Executive Edi-
tor of Ministry Resources
Jim Townsend, Bible Editor
Gregory Eaton Clark, Director of
Design Services

■

Scripture quotations, unless otherwise
noted, are from the *Holy Bible: New In-
ternational Version.* © 1978 New York
International Bible Society. Used by
permission of Zondervan Bible
Publishers.
*We'd like to thank the many
encouragers who helped PACESETTER
become reality. —The Editors*
Published by David C. Cook Publishing
Co.
850 North Grove Avenue
Elgin, Illinois 60120
Cable address: DCCOOK
Second printing, October 1986
Printed in the United States of America
Library of Congress Catalog Card Num-
ber: 85-72934
ISBN: 0-89191-329-7

Cover photo by Bakstad Photographics

Life Choices

TACKLING THE BIGGEST DECISIONS YOU'LL MAKE

Once every 90 minutes a young person makes the choice to take his or her own life. Kids are making choices all the time about less ultimate issues, like friends, jobs, music, clothes, sexual activity, drug use, etc. As caring adult friends we can have a significant influence on the life choices our teenagers are making. We must remember that when we feel overwhelmed or helpless in the face of cultural pressures on kids.

We can help our young people by giving them tools and processes to make both personal as well as vocational life choices. We can start by remembering some of our own feelings of uncertainty as we confronted difficult choices when we were teenagers. Do you remember anyone who offered you words of assurance and encouragement, or who listened and guided you in making some of your important decisions? If you can, you can translate some of your experiences and feelings into action now as you deal with kids who need your understanding and advice.

Life choices force us to consider what is of ultimate importance to us. Teenagers are no exception. Because they are being challenged to the core, they are more open to looking at questions of meaning and purpose. Maybe that's why so many young people are open to Christ in a unique way during these years. And maybe that's the greatest gift you have to offer them—your experience of the security and guidance that only the Holy Spirit can give.

INSIDE · THIS · VOLUME

LIFE CHOICES: Tackling the Biggest Decisions You'll Make (Volume Five in the PACESETTER series) can help you guide the kids in your group through the many decisions they will face in the next few years.

First, for background on the topic and your own enrichment, we offer "Expert Insights," articles by leaders in youth ministry. For example, *Youth Letter* editor, Jim Reapsome, takes a hard look at the complex choices facing today's youth. J. David Stone talks about how, as significant adults, we can help our young people make wise decisions. And Philip Yancey questions our assumptions about how God guides us.

Then, use PACESETTER's practical programming tools:

■ The "Meetings" section gives you five complete meeting plans on some of the basic kinds of choices kids face—vocation, life partners, and lifestyle. Reproduce the activity pieces at the back of this book for use with these meetings.

■ Then there's the "More Bright Ideas" section. Here you'll find around 20 activity ideas, many suitable as meetings in themselves. Use them whenever you need them.

■ How about a progressive dinner where kids and adults mingle to get to know each other and discuss the kinds of choices the adults have made? Check out the "Breakaway" section.

■ Turn to the "Kids in the Spotlight" section for a puppet skit that pokes fun at the ways we sometimes go about making decisions.

■ Finally, to help you build a coherent, supportive group identity, we've included "Nurturing Your Group" by Dr. Gary Downing.

Ready to go? Good. You've made the right choice. □

Contents

Inside
This Volume

3

Expert
Insights

*A Look at
This Volume's Topic
By Leaders in Youth
Ministry*

Finding the
Will of God:
No Magic Formulas

By Philip Yancey

6

Tough Choices

By James Reapsome

12

Big Decisions

By J. David Stone

18

Meetings

*A Variety of
Complete Meetings
On This
Volume's
Topic*

Decisions,
Decisions,
Decisions

By Dave Veerman

20

Finding God's Will

By Dave Veerman

24

Create a Date;
Find a Mate

By Sue Toman

28

Keep Up the Good
Work!

By Rick and Ellen
Thompson

32

Contents

What's Money
For?

By Sandy Larsen

36

More
Bright
Ideas

A Grab Bag of Ideas
On the Volume's Topic

Activity
Ideas on the
Theme, 'Choices'

By Dave Veerman

40

Nurturing
Your Group

An Article and
Activities to
Build Your Group

Dealing with
Conflict

By Gary W. Downing

46

Kids In The
Spotlight

A Skit,
Puppet Script, Drama,
Or Worship Service

My Choices . . .
Which Voices?

A puppet script

By Dale VonSeggen

48

Breakaway

A Retreat,
Lock-in, Work Camp,
Or Travel Idea
For Outside
Your Group's
Regular Setting

Grub and Gab

A Unique Dinner for Kids
And Adults

By Marlene D. LeFever

52

Activity
Pieces

A Variety of Handouts
To Use in Meetings
And Retreats

57

How does an infinite God guide finite human beings? Or does He even bother?

Finding the Will of God: No Magic Formulas

The issues are immediate

and clear cut. Who do I marry? What job should I take? Should I go to a Christian or secular college? Which church should I attend? Ought I consider having another child? Should I move to Texas? Each of us has a customized set of these questions that hover oppressively over our daily routines.

It would seem reasonable to expect God to be involved in such major decisions affecting our lives. And yet, try to make sense, if you will, of the most commonly heard advice on the topic of divine guidance.

BY PHILIP YANCEY

Mystical Guidance

————■————

The older strain of advice has a more mystical or supernatural aura about it. Some Christians teach that God has a plan for each of our lives, a wonderful plan, in fact, and that we only need discover it to know what school we should attend, who we should marry, what occupation we should choose, where we should live. God's plan is individual and specific. For direction on how to decipher the recondite secrets of this plan, these Christians turn to such examples as Gideon's putting out a fleece and Paul's vision of a Macedonian call. To me, the selection of those two examples has always seemed curious in the extreme.

In the story reported in Judges 6 and 7, Gideon clearly emerges as an example of doubt and vacillation. Has anyone experienced such irrefutable guidance? After a personal visit from an angel of God, who gave exact instructions, Gideon asked for and got a confirming sign: the spontaneous combustion of his offering to the Lord. Still nervous about the military improbability of his task, he asked for another sign, that of a wet fleece. When that was provided, he had the audacity to ask for yet a third sign, the dry fleece. After all these supernatural confirmations, Gideon still shrank from his task until God recommended he stroll among the tents of the enemy and listen to their conversations.

"Putting out the fleece" hardly seems an appropriate model for someone seeking guidance. It better describes someone who knows exactly what God wants and still quakes before the task.

Similarly, the account of the Macedonian call offers a dubious prototype for guidance. The most evident fact is that this vision came as such a surprise to Paul. He planned his missionary journeys as strategically as a general plans army maneuvers. But this one time (Acts 16:6-10), he ran into a roadblock. "The spirit of Jesus" constrained him from his determined route and the vision suggested an alternative. In a survey of the Book of Acts to discern Paul's reliance on guidance, the Macedonian call stands out as a spectacular aberration from normal experience—hardly the type of incident to construct a philosophy of guidance around.

Rational Guidance

————■————

Lately, a more pragmatic school of thinking about guidance has sprung up in Christian circles. A sincere questioner uses such resources as the Bible, the inner promptings of the Holy Spirit, and external circumstances to descry God's will. "Line up those three like harbor lights," a popular analogy advises, "and your ship safely glides in." Some add a fourth harbor light: the wise counsel of fellow Christians. In essence, this strain of thought has made the whole issue of guidance less mysterious, more rational.

Very recently a more iconoclastic school of thought has appeared. A book called *Decision Making and the Will of God* by Garry Friesen has sold 100,000 copies and stirred up considerable controversy. He spends the first few chapters developing a caricature of a pastor who gives seminars on traditionally accepted notions of guidance. Then Friesen asks a major question. Does God, in fact, have an "individual will" for me that specifies in advance the major choices in my life? Friesen concludes that God has a moral will, fully revealed in the Bible. But where no specific command or principle is given, the believer is free and responsible to choose his or her own course of action. Friesen devotes 452 pages to proving his point.

Some Examination

————■————

How, then, can we deal with the major anxieties about the future that hang over us? Whereas some Christians exhort us to seek a deep, mystical confirmation before deciding on a course of action, others admonish us to study the Bible and then make up our own minds. Where do we look for guidance to help decide on a philosophy of guidance?

Frankly, for various reasons I have found these common approaches confusing and at least partly unsatisfying. They often leave unanswered basic questions about God's sovereignty and His readiness to impinge on human affairs. In thinking about guidance, I have tried to take a step back from the actual precipice of choice in order to consider more fundamental questions of how an infinite God could guide finite human beings. "What are His options?" I have asked myself (knowing full well that questions phrased like that are hopelessly inadequate when one contemplates an infinite God). In this process, I have relied on a wonderful, although densely written, philosophical work entitled *Incarnation and Immanence* by Lady Helen Oppenheimer. The book is unavailable in an American edition, so I will try to compensate by freely borrowing some of its seminal ideas.

Lady Oppenheimer begins her discussion on divine guidance by first examining how we ask other human beings for guidance. What do we ask for when we ask for guidance? She lists three common examples.

1. We ask some people's support of the decision we are already leaning toward. Employees within large companies do this masterfully by seeking counsel with precisely those people who will build a ground swell of support for their own pet projects. Children are even more disingenuous: they

to make his or her own decisions. The counselor takes on a long-term goal of freeing the client from the unhealthy dependency of "victimization."

The counselor's response offers an important insight into one of the most puzzling aspects of the whole guidance issue. Why does not God forthrightly tell me which decision is the right one? Could it be because such a response would

restating our opinions. Lady Helen Oppenheimer expresses the frustration this way, "One cannot go on forever being grateful for silence. A good listener is not one who we begin to think has gone quietly away." And we do, after all, want guidance, not just sympathy, from an all-knowing God.

Guidance and God's Omniscience

These examples of human guidance can only begin to express the "problem" of an infinite God guiding finite human beings. Consider, for example, a healthy form of human guidance that falls under the second category of Oppenheimer's list. We consult experts in fields such as law or medicine, freely subjecting ourselves to their superior judgment on issues of vital importance. We want, and pay dearly for, their informed advice. Is not an omniscient God an ideal "expert," fully informed on the particulars of our lives, and the most objective adviser we could possibly imagine?

At this point, the difference between finitude and infinitude crops up. I go to a lawyer or a doctor in order to exhaust his advice. I want him to study books, talk to his colleagues, scan his computer files to gather the best possible advice. He helps me to the limits of his capacity. When he is done, I take the results and make the decision on my course of action.

With God, it is different. He has unlimited capacity. In a curious sort of way, it would be cheating at the most basic level of human independence to receive "the inside story" of how the future will turn out. There would be no meaningful opportunity for faith or obedience if I knew the inevitable

> *He desires not so much to run our lives as to have us, in full control of our lives, offer them to Him in obedience and service.*

possess an instinctive ability to sense which parent will most likely agree with their desires, and approach that parent for permission.

But surely this common technique does not offer us a model for asking advice of God. Going to Him for approval of our predetermined ideas and plans would be sheer blasphemy. We must look to other models.

2. We go to some people because we truly want to be *told* what to do. "I can't decide which college to go to—*you* tell me," the befuddled teenager asks his parents. "Look, it's up to you whether we have another child or not," says one spouse. "You decide, and I'll go along with whatever you choose."

Professional counselors encounter this type of questioner often; the indecisiveness itself is the reason for the counseling. Such clients yearn for a wise parent to make all the important decisions in life. A wise counselor rears back from playing a direct parental role. The client needs not good advice, but the mature ability

inevitably jeopardize human freedom, a course God has scrupulously avoided taking from the Garden of Eden onward? He desires not so much to run our lives as to have us, in full control of our lives, offer them to Him in obedience and service. (I am speaking here of morally neutral issues. Anything revealed in Scripture needs no further guidance initiative; it is God's Word to us.)

3. Sometimes we simply want a chance to think aloud, in the presence of a friendly listener. Whole schools of therapy have arisen to extol the virtues of such a role. The counselor should nod meaningfully, restate the client's questions for him or her, and essentially help the client clarify a position without directive interference.

At first glance, the "friendly listener" approach does resemble our approach to the divine in prayer. But there are crucial differences, too. In prayer we have no visible proof of anyone listening, not even the bare minimum of a person nodding a head and result of taking one sort of action and not another. Human freedom would dissolve. An all-knowing God cannot "give advice" like a conscientious lawyer. Where does He draw the line? Imagine what would happen if one musician (or one politician, or one pastor, or one confused college student), but not others, had direct and limitless access to God's infinite wisdom and creativity. The rules governing the whole planet would shift.

C. S. Lewis hinted at God's hesitance to intervene directly: "He seems to do nothing of Himself which He can possibly delegate to His creatures. He commands us to do slowly and blunderingly what He could do perfectly and in the twinkling of an eye . . . . Perhaps we do not fully realize the problem, so to call it, of enabling finite free wills to coexist with Omnipotence. It seems to involve at every moment almost a sort of 'divine abdication.' "

Let me summarize the problem of "divine abdication" by referring back to Lady Oppenheimer's three models for human guidance. It seems common forms of human guidance take on grave difficulties when God Himself is the other party. Surely we do not want to use Him as a rubber stamp on decisions (option one). He cannot easily fill the role of an objective "friendly listener" (option three) for paradoxical reasons: because of His invisible spirit nature and also because of His own unlimited capacity and omniscience.

The second example of guidance, that of "telling us what to do," is probably the least likely avenue God will take, out of respect for human freedom. There are exceptions, of course, the Macedonian call and Gideon's fleece being among them; but these stand out primarily because they are exceptions. Perhaps we have the key here as to why the

issue of guidance causes so much frustration among Christians. Of the various alternatives, is not this the one we secretly desire—that of being told in our prayers what to do? And yet God, with good reason, usually refrains from guiding so directly.

Does God Guide?

— ■ —

Most discussions on guidance tend to vaporize at about this point in the argument. We are very good at defining what guidance is not, but very bad at defining what it is. I began with the personal issues of choice that hang over each of us, and I cannot go on forever pointing out the problems in divine guidance. To be honest, I must somehow address the practical matter involving God in the decision-making process.

Yet I have begun to wonder if our problem with guidance centers in our tendency to see it in terms of a technique, rather than as part of a relationship. As techniques, the first and third examples presented by Lady Oppenheimer

fail to satisfy, but seen in the context of a relationship they take on an entirely different light.

I think of the most intimate relationship I have ever had, that of marriage for 13 years to my wife, Janet. I quickly confess that in this human relationship, also, Oppenheimer's second option is the rarest: I almost never go to my wife to be told what to do. But, within the womb of intimacy, I do

often go to her to seek support for my own decisions (option one) and to seek out a compassionate "friendly listener" who has my best interests at heart (option three).

At times in the rush of the day, I have neglected to mention some important fact, even a pleasing thing that has happened to me, perhaps an article that has been accepted for publication or an award. If my wife finds out later, she confronts me with a wounded, sometimes fiery look. "You never told me that!" she accuses. She should know more about me than anyone else—hers is an entirely appropriate, even endearing, kind of jealousy.

Or, I think of negative things in our marriage: an irritation I try to bury deep inside, a necessary confrontation I seek to avoid, a fear or insecurity I wish would go away. After 13 years, I have simply given up trying to hide those things from Janet. They will come out sometime, maybe weeks later, maybe months. My own body will give me away: a tilt of the jaw, a

> *There would be no meaningful oppor-tunity for faith or obedience if I knew the inevitable result of taking one sort of action and not another.*

quiver of the eye, a sudden stiffening, an unnatural silence.

The very *fact* of communication is almost as important as the content of it. In one sense, I almost never go to Janet "for advice" on an issue—not, at least, in the way I would go to a lawyer or professional counselor for advice. But in another sense, everything that I do and that I am I strive to share with her. When I do face a choice between two options, naturally I go through the process with her. But at the end, when the decision is reached, we are both quite unsure of who contributed what to the ultimate result. Such a division—who contributes what—would seem strangely irrelevant to intimacy. Certainly we both maintain our independence in the process, and yet somehow—if we are relating healthily—we arrive at a truly joint decision.

In the intimacy of human marriage, perhaps we can catch a glimpse of the intimacy longed for by God. A theme peals out from the Bible, a ringing of bells, a call for us humans to act like the Bride of Christ that we are. God is the lover, we the beloved. When we reject Him, we prostitute ourselves—the sexual imagery fills the prophetic books.

Here is an important clue: The Bible contains very little specific advice on the techniques of guidance, but very much on the proper way to maintain a love relationship with God. What Janet and I are learning—the small and large communications that make up our life together—is a shadow of intimacy God desires from me. He wants a conscious and willing acceptance of His presence whenever I make a decision. The spotlight of guidance shifts from technique to relationship.

The Psalms And Guidance

— ■ —

If someone asked me for a recommendation of a Biblical text on the doctrine of guidance, I would quickly suggest the Psalms. Yes, that's right, all 150 of them. I learned to appreciate the Psalms on a trip to Colorado, in the midst of the busiest and most anxiety-filled year of my life. I had to go

somewhere to escape office pressures in order to concentrate on one last editing of a book manuscript, and I chose Colorado in the month of May. I also needed to seek out guidance on some major decisions about my future.

I determined to arise early each morning, drive or walk to a scenic setting, and begin the day by reading, in order, straight through ten psalms. Those mornings still stand out with all the bracing clarity of the morning mountain air. Clusters of bright green aspen trees were coming into leaf, staining the sheltered folds of the still-wintry mountains with a gash of life. I would stare around me for a long time before reading.

Previously, I had dipped into the Psalms one at a time, finding a familiar one here or there. I found the technique of reading ten in sequence jarring. Some of them offered praise to God in jubilation and thanksgiving. They extolled His everlasting love, His deliverance, His clear guidance in daily affairs. Others, often sandwiched in between the most triumphant ones, blasted God for His seeming absence, His failure to guide clearly, His apparent forgetfulness of the promises He had made. At first the discord seemed bizarre, almost as if the Hebrew canonizers had arranged the order with a streak of mocking irony.

After a few days of unresolved dissonance, I began to change my perspective on the Psalms. I stopped looking to them for specific advice and instead viewed

them as spiritual journals, accounts of a few people who took seriously the intimate relationship between God and man. The authors were brutally honest, chronicling the full benefits of that love relationship, but also the outrageous disappointments. (Martin Marty, in his recent book *Cry of Absence,* characterizes one-half of Psalms as "wintry" ones and only one-third as summery ones. You must read

> *There is no shortcut, no magic. There is only the possibility of a lifetime search for intimacy with God.*

all 150 to get the full picture, the welter of emotions and faith and doubt.)

The putative author of some of those psalms was called "a man after God's own heart." I now understand why. In his life, David always took God seriously. He intentionally involved God in every minor and major triumph and every minor and major failure. He railed at God, exalted Him, doubted Him, praised Him, feared Him, loved Him. But regardless of what happened, God was never far from David's thoughts. David practiced the presence of God in daily details, and then took the time to keep a revealing poetic record of the intimacy between them. The repetitive, even tedious, prosody of the Psalms is perhaps their main point. They primarily communicate not concepts, but rather the record of how a relationship is maintained.

Not Magic, but Faith

— ■ —

I confess that I have shifted tracks in the middle of an article, but I have done so because I believe most of the questions about guidance, the "how-to's" are misdirected. They are the typically impatient demands of us Americans who want a shortcut to the "magic," the benefit of relating to almighty God. There is no shortcut, no magic—at least not that anyone can reduce to a three-point outline. There is only the possibility of a lifetime search for intimacy with a God who, as the psalmists discovered, sometimes seems close and sometimes far, sometimes seems loving and sometimes forgetful. We have little sympathy, as Lewis said, for the "problems" of Omnipotence. But God does not want sympathy, He wants love and a lasting commitment to take Him seriously, every day, regardless. And if there is a formula for guidance, it would have to be that.

Does God guide? Yes, I believe that He does. Most times, I believe, He guides in subtle ways,

by feeding ideas into our minds, speaking through a nagging sensation of dissatisfaction, inspiring us to choose better than we otherwise would have done, bringing to the surface hidden dangers of temptation, and perhaps by rearranging certain circumstances. (He may also still guide through visions, dreams, and prophetic utterances, but I cannot speak to these forms as they lie outside my field of experience.) God's guidance will supply real help, but in ways that will not overwhelm my freedom.

And yet, I cannot help thinking this whole issue of divine guidance, which draws throngs of seekers to seminars and sells thousands of books, is powerfully overrated. It deserves about as much attention as the Bible devotes to the topic.

The sociologist Bronislaw Malinowski suggested a distinction between magic and religion.

Magic, he said, is when we manipulate the deities so that they perform our wishes; religion is when we subject ourselves to the will of the deities. True guidance cannot resemble magic, a way for God to give shortcuts and genie bottles. It must, rather, fall under Malinowski's definition of religion. If so, it will occur in the context of a committed relationship between a Christian and his God. Once that relationship exists, divine guidance becomes not an end in itself but merely one more means God uses in nourishing faith. □

Philip Yancey, former editor of Campus Life *magazine, is author of several popular books, such as* Where Is God When It Hurts? *(Zondervan). He writes from his home in Chicago, Illinois. From the book,* Guidance by Philip Yancey, *© 1983 by Philip Yancey. Published by Multnomah Press, Portland, Oregon 97266. Used by permission.*

To Choose or Not to Choose. . .

To not choose is itself a choice. It's a choice to yield control of your will and actions to someone or something other than yourself.

"Most people fail in the art of living not because they are inherently bad or so without will that they cannot lead a better life," Psychologist Erich Fromm has written, "they fail because they do not wake up and see when they stand at a fork in the road and have to decide. They are not aware when life asks them a question, and when they still have alternative answers.

Then with each step along the wrong road it becomes increasingly difficult for them to admit that they are on the wrong road, often only because they have to admit that they must go back to the first wrong turn, and must accept the fact that they have wasted energy and time."

I can recall many times when Fromm's statement has described me perfectly. It's very difficult to break a chain of wrong choices. But it is possible, with God's help. And it's also possible to begin a new

chain of right choices that, over the long haul, will make your life better than you could have imagined.

Ultimately, God is in control. But he has given you much more control, more power, more freedom and more responsibility than you might think. Can you handle it?

From Campus Life, *"Your Freedom to Choose" by* Verne Becker, *September, 1984.*

□

Tough Choices

Today's teenagers worry about the world of tomorrow.

A look at the choices facing today's youth

They see not only international dilemmas begging solutions, but also problems closer to home: unemployment, family breakdown, their parents' mid-life crises, and corruption in government and business. They see people hurting deeply because of divorce, abuse, poverty, and economic dislocation. They fear that today's auto worker being replaced by a robot could be one of them in the future being knocked out of a job by the next generation of scientific discoveries.

BY JIM REAPSOME

Today's youth sense the depersonalization in the work place, the uncertainty of social security, and the influence of computers on more and more of life. Above all, they are convinced that they will have to make lots of money. Polls of entering-college freshmen show, year after year, that success in their careers and financial security rank at the top of their list of goals.

Education and a Career

Life's big decisions are being forced on youth at a time when they feel it's unfair for them to choose. But once they enter the fast lane in high school, they must choose courses and majors that will set the direction of their future education and careers. Even with the help of computers to sort out options, students are baffled simply because the world of the late twentieth century offers them a bewildering array of choices.

I recall encountering the multiplicity of choices in our children's high school catalogs. In scope, it far eclipsed what I had to choose from in college. Electives covered every conceivable area of interest.

Even the very first step after high school frightens many 18-year-olds. If college, which one? How can I pay for it? If my parents can't afford to help, how will I be able to repay the loans? If not college, what kind of work? What about the military? What about "full-time" Christian service? Many college-bound, high school seniors are torn between picking a Christian college or a state university. They hear conflicting advice at home and at church. Somehow, the pastor's sermons on guidance and finding God's will make it sound much simpler than it really is. Well-meaning adults nudge them to be sure they know God's will. Meanwhile, prevailing culture tells them to aim for the most prestigious school and to choose a career that will bring the highest financial rewards and social status.

Choosing a Life Partner

It's been said that next to choosing Christ as Savior and Lord, the most crucial decision a person makes is that of a life partner. Youth surveys tell us that the vast majority of teens anticipate marriage, and they think of it as a lasting commitment. On the other hand, perhaps half of them have already been victimized by their parents' divorces. Many teen behavioral problems can be traced to the trauma of divorce. It's not unusual for teenagers to be living in either single-parent or blended families (with second or third fathers or mothers, or with live-in men or women).

Therefore, although teens have not lost the ideal of marriage, they do seem afraid of failure because

> Teens see the phoniness in adults who pay lip service to traditional prohibitions but fail to live up to them.

of all the wreckage they see around them. I once overheard two girls talking in a college snack shop. One was admonishing the other to be sure to get her degree and some good job experience before getting married, because divorce was sure to follow and she would then need to be able to make it on her own. Statistically, she was right.

Although teenagers tell poll-takers that they believe marriage should last, deep down they are practical enough to know that the chances for that happening are slim. They know there is an escape hatch—divorce—which carries with it little, if any, social disapproval. They know that today's prevailing attitude is that everyone's inalienable right is to be happy, and if a marriage interferes with that right, then the marriage commitment must bow before a higher priority.

Daily Moral Choices

All teens feel tension about making choices that they know will affect their futures. They also worry about choices that they must make every day. These choices concern three areas.

1. *Sex*. The choice to abstain must be made against a tidal wave of pressure to enjoy sexual gratification now, rather than waiting until marriage.

Why is this choice so hard to make? For one thing, teens see the phoniness in adults who pay lip service to traditional prohibitions against fornication and adultery but fail to live up to them.

Another reason is peer pressure. Joan Lipsitz, Director of the Center for Early Adolescence, gives these statistics for unmarried teenagers: 12 percent of 13-year-old males and 2 percent of 13-year-old females are sexually active. The percentage increases each year so that by age 18, 70 percent of the males and 52 percent of the females are sexually active (*Common Focus*, Vol. 6, No. 1, 1985, p. 2). In many cases, if a young person does not have sex, he or she feels like a social pariah.

The advertising and entertainment worlds also drive home powerful sexual messages. They use sex to sell their products. This constant stimulation makes it more difficult for young people to control their sexual urges. It also confuses their sense of values by glorifying promiscuity.

In addition to all of these pressures, homosexual-rights groups make strong pitches to teenagers. They advertise gay hot lines which tell teens to shop around and experiment with a number of sexual partners. Many teens face honest doubts about their own sexuality, and the drift into homosexual liaisons is made easier by society's increasing acceptance of homosexuality as a normal human condition.

2. *Drugs and Alcohol.* A confusing array of choices confronts teenagers with regard to drugs and alcohol. Deciding to smoke marijuana has been made easier because it is easy to get and the law usually looks the other way. Surveys show that overall use of marijuana by teenagers has declined slightly, but their use of cocaine has increased slightly.

Teen drinking—because of its link with traffic fatalities—has aroused nationwide concern. To choose not to drink is tough, in some cases because parents often approve of drinking as an acceptable alternative to drugs.

3. *Entertainment.* Some social scientists say that the strongest influence on teen choices arises out of the entertainment world: movies, music, television, and magazines. For example, pop

> **Inextricably entwined with every decision teens have to make is the choice to live or die.**

singer Michael Jackson's attire was seen in every high school in America at the height of his popularity.

Movie producers have hit the jackpot with films pandering to the lowest side of life. While the public's boundaries of decency have been plundered by the entertainment world, the churches by and large have remained silent. Teens know that the rating system for movies is rarely, if ever, enforced at the box office. Many of them are left completely on their own when making entertainment choices.

Almost by default, many young people feel forced to accept whatever the entertainment world offers them. The lack of viable alternatives contributes strongly to their surrender, especially in regard to movies and television. In the absence of clear-cut "thou shalt nots," counselors of teenagers must recognize that music, movies, rock video, and television are ripe subjects for discussion.

Teenagers need and appreciate guidance about the Biblical principles and values that underlie

wise entertainment choices. But adding to the complexity of those choices is the fact that families within the same church often hold different standards about what is acceptable entertainment and what is not.

The Choice to Live or Die

— ■ —

Inextricably entwined with every decision teens have to make is the choice to live or die.

Brian Hiemer came from a good, rural family. He had a 3.3 grade point average. He was a starter for the University of Nebraska football team. The day before fall practice was to start, he shot himself to death on his father's farm.

Every year about 5,000 teenagers choose to die. That's triple the suicide rate for teens 30 years ago. Rich kids and poor kids take their own lives, high achievers and dropouts, rural kids and city kids.

Why this rise in suicides? The possibility of a nuclear holocaust, terrorist suicide bombings, and mass starvation—to say nothing of television's consistent portrayal of people being "blown away" in real life as well as in fiction—cause today's youth to wonder whether or not the world is a fit place to grow up in. The aimlessness and sham of much of what the world counts as important also load the deck in favor of suicide.

In addition to those reasons, the complexity of the choices which high school students face adds to their sense of hopelessness and to their fear of being unable to cope with the pressures of modern life. Often a divorce in the family, the death of a friend or family member, or even breaking up with a boyfriend or girlfriend, provides the spark that ignites a fatally wrong choice.

Choices in Christian Context

— ■ —

The biggest decisions in their lives lie ahead for today's high school youth. For all the fun they seem to be having, they do worry about those choices. Their fears are compounded by the complexity of choices and by the lack of clearly established moral boundaries in the adult world. The Bible's clearly intoned, "This is the way, walk in it," is but a dim vision from some distant planet light-years in the past.

Teens have many fears about growing up in the topsy-turvy world they see all around them. Add to that their everyday worries about what to wear, how to get enough money for clothes, dates, and cars, and what to do for excitement, and you can understand why they need ample opportunities for friendly Christian counsel and brainstorming in the context of the Church.

Even when they are under intense pain and conflict, they must see that life is indeed worth living—not for themselves alone—but for others who love them, for those in the world who need them, for God who created them, and for Jesus Christ who redeemed them.

□

Jim Reapsome *is the founder and editor of Youth Letter. He is also the editor of* Evangelical Missions Quarterly. *He has spoken at numerous youth camps and retreats.*

Today's Youth — A statistical portrait

Schooling: The National Center for Education Statistics (NCES) estimates that for every 100 pupils who were in the fifth grade in fall 1972, 99 entered ninth grade in 1976, 89 entered eleventh grade in 1978, and 75 graduated from high school in 1980.

The dropout rate appears to be about the same among black and white 14- to 17-year-olds, around 5.3 percent in October 1979; for 18- to 21-year-olds, however, the white dropout rate is 15.5 percent and the black dropout rate is 25.5 percent.

Employment: According to the Bureau of Labor Statistics, approximately 48 percent of teenagers had jobs in 1960; in 1979, almost 60 percent worked. According to NCES, 63 percent of high school seniors and 42 percent of sophomores had paying jobs in 1980.

Again, we can interpret these figures in various ways. On the one hand, today's youth are clearly not rejecting the work ethic. In fact, in 1980, 88 percent of high school seniors said that being successful in their line of work was very important to them, up 4 percent since 1972, and 84 percent said finding steady work was very important, up 6 percent.

On the other hand, at least one-third of all young people will work at fast-food restaurants when they are teenagers, in low-wage, tedious, dead-end, and sometimes dangerous jobs. For some adolescents, numerous hours of work may lead to lowered grades . . . and other disturbing behavior. And much more troubling are the statistics about black youth. The proportion of black teenagers in the work force decreased from 45 percent in 1960 to 41 percent in 1979. For black males, the decrease is marked, from 44 percent to 30 percent. Hispanic teenagers appear to be faring better. In 1979, 50 percent of Hispanic teenagers held jobs.

Sexual Activity: Evidence indicates an increase in sexual activity among adolescents but a downward trend in adolescent childbearing. In 1960 the birthrate per 1,000 women aged 15 to 19 was 89.1. That number has steadily decreased. In 1978 it was 52.4. But "while the teenage birthrate has been declining, the incidence of out-of-wedlock births among teenagers has been increasing. In 1978, over one-half of all births to teenagers were to women who were unmarried, compared to 17 percent in 1960" [Mark Testa and Fred Wulczyn, *The State of the Child,* The Children's Policy Research Project, Vol. I, p. 29].

The death rate among mothers from complications during pregnancy and childbirth is 13 percent greater for 15- to 19-year-olds than for women in their twenties. For teenagers under age 15, the death rate is 60 percent greater.

From Common Focus *(Vol. 6, No. 1, 1985). Reprinted by permission of The Center for Early Adolescence.*

Youth Unemployment

How youth leaders can help fight it.

Unemployment has challenged every facet of life in England during the past five years. Churches first reached out to youth by opening their doors and establishing "drop-in" centers. Eventually the kids were asking for advice on a wide range of subjects, leading us to establish "advice centers." Sometimes two or three neighborhood churches join together to staff an advice center for unemployed youth. The advisers are volunteers; many have been trained by a national citizens advisory group. Churches work with local industries to sponsor part-time youth work; the sponsoring client pays for all materials. Sometimes the kids are paid, sometimes not.

Similar projects could be duplicated in the U.S. Youth groups could hire themselves out to firms or community service organizations or churches to do painting, window washing, landscaping, etc. Individual teens could train as pastoral assistants—visiting the elderly, doing clerical work, assisting in Sunday school—in exchange for room and board and a minimal amount of spending money.

Youth involved in projects with professional craftsmen receive valuable (and marketable) training. Youth working for community organizations are contributing to society, which elicits personal pride and satisfaction. The youth gain job experience. The different jobs that a youth group undertakes can help kids decide what they might like to do on a full-time basis, what kind of further training they need, etc.

From Campus Life, *December 1984*

Youth Values

Values influence decision making. A study by Search Institute revealed the ten things most valued by the ninth graders they surveyed:
1. Get a good job
2. Have happy family life
3. Do something important
4. Feel good about myself
5. Have friends I can count on
6. Do well in school
7. Make parents proud
8. Live in world without war
9. Have fun and good times
10. Have God at center of my life

Adapted from Young Adolescents and Their Parents, *a 1984 report by Search Institute, 122 West Franklin Ave., Suite 525, Minneapolis, MN 55404.*

□

When the Going Gets Tough . . .

According to a recent study by the National Urban League, life continues to be stacked against the typical black male. For him, unemployment hovers around the 14 percent mark (for white males, the figure is 6 percent). And for those who do find work, the average income is $10,510, while white men earn an average of $15,373.

Although blacks no longer have to sit at the backs of buses, they are stifled by more subtle forms of discrimination. From childhood on, whether they are openly mistreated or simply ignored, the message is clear: "I don't expect you to amount to much." As a result, many blacks come to think so little of themselves that they are, in a sense, crippled and robbed of hope.

Getting a college education is one way out, of course. But the problem of low expectations remains. "People have preconceptions about what a black person is supposed to be," says James Borders, editor of *The Black Collegian* magazine. "That often means poor, ghetto bred, prone to violence—and not as academically gifted as whites."

Consequently, many minority students assume early on that they're not college material and don't bother to take the kinds of courses they need for college. Too often, counselors let them get away with this attitude, too. *Reprint permission granted by* Campus Voice *magazine: copyright 1986.*

Big Decisions

Helping

youth

make

life

choices

"*D*ad,
I'm engaged! I'm going to be married!"

My heart stopped. I had known that one day this was going to happen. I was even happy, I think . . .

"You don't sound happy for me," she said.

"Of course I am!" I replied. But secretly I knew that she was right. I did not sound happy. I was puzzled. Why? Her fiance *had* talked to me three days before and asked for my blessing and I had assured him that I would be happy to have him as a son-in-law. Mitzi had completed college and Peter was a successful attorney. Then why, why would I not sound happy for her?

As I pondered this question, I realized that it was one of the most important decisions she would ever make and I wanted it to be the *right one.*

Life choices are tough! They are for *life!* And I believe the chance for happiness increases as those choices are made correctly.

Tough Choices for Youth

■

Statistics show that between the ages of 17 and 23 we make the most important decisions of our lives:

■ Who our permanent friends will be.

■ Where or if we are going to college.

■ Who, or if, or when we will marry.

■ What career we will pursue.

■ Where we stand in our own faith.

No wonder it is vital for those of us who work with high schoolers to be in touch with not only the youth of today, but with ourselves and our own faith.

B Y   J.   D A V I D   S T O N E

Their Own Decisions

Individual youth must make their own decisions. We cannot and *must* not make those important decisions for them. Oh, I know, we usually know what is best, but the decision does not have a chance if we make it for them. We want to help kids profit from our mistakes. But we do not have all the data that is necessary to make the complete decision.

Since high schoolers have the data about themselves, rather than try to tell them which button to push, we should teach kids *how* to decide for themselves.

Significant Adults

Most of us are significant adults in teens' lives. I remember Coach Nichols. I would have run through a wall had he asked me. He had a great influence on my life. As I reflect, I can remember him *being there* for me. He did not make decisions for me, but he set the parameters of what it meant to be a good football player: "You train hard, give that extra lap after practice, don't let your ego rule, and always do your best!"

Having that kind of motivation from someone I respected, I had choices to make. I could drink–and break training rules–or keep my-self fit. I could slough off in practice or give extra. I could talk about how good I was or let my actions speak. It was up to me to be my best or not. We need to challenge youth to be the best that they can be. That is one way to teach them how to make decisions while not telling them what decisions to make.

To help youth make critical life choices, we must first build significant relationships with them. This means spending time getting to know youth in as many arenas of their lives as possible. Not only should we see them or visit with them at the church, but also in their homes, their school environment, and in places they hang out.

As youth begin to know us, trust and influence grow. And when we really know a young person, we have an understanding of who he or she is, and we *may* be able to help when he or she hurts. Then, by our example and the story of our experiences, we can help youth make their own decisions. Studies indicate that youth tend to emulate their significant adult. Though it seems unfair to put us in such a position, we, as youth workers, *must* be the best we can be.

Our Own Decisions

I have a hunch that it would do us good to simply look at ourselves and learn from the experiences we had in making our important life choices. Our sensitivity to what youth are experiencing can tremendously increase the impact that we can have in their lives.

Take some time to reflect on your life choices by thinking through your answers to the following questions. They may help you remember how tough it was when *you* were making some of those choices!

■ How old was I when I first began thinking about getting married? my career? which college I would attend or if I would attend at all?

■ How did my views on these things change as I got older? What caused those changes? With whom did I share my feelings?

■ Who gave me the best advice?

■ What influence did my family background have?

■ What natural (physical, emotional, etc.) considerations came into play?

■ Did a part-time job encourage or discourage me?

■ How did my responsibilities at home affect any of these decisions?

■ Did my friends try to influence me? How much influence did they have?

■ What part did my pastor or youth worker play? Was I grateful or resentful?

■ Did I let God have a part in my decisions? How? How do I feel about that now?

Now, before you make suggestions to your kids, check *your* answers to these questions.

Helping Kids

By getting to know our youth, by becoming vulnerable to them in sharing about our lives, by being sensitive to what kids are going through, and by being the best examples possible, we can help our kids with their most important life choices. The choices they have to make will not be that much easier, but youth can at least have a little greater chance of being right. □

J. David Stone lectures at Centenary College and is executive director of Youth Ministries Consultation Service. He has written several youth ministry books, and leads workshops for youth workers across the United States.

Aim

Overview

You'll Need

Decisions, Decisions, Decisions

To help young people understand and use a mature decision-making process. Key passages: Proverbs 3:5, 6; Hebrews 11:6.

Our lives are the sum of the decisions we make. It is important, therefore, to be able to make mature choices instead of being moved and formed by the decisions of others. And for Christians, God must be at the center of this decision-making process. This meeting helps kids think about the decisions they have to make and examine some Biblical guidelines for making them. It works best when followed by the meeting, ''Finding God's Will,'' also found in this book.

1. Making Choices (Games) 10-15 min.
   Activity 1
   □ poster board   □ rulers
   □ magic markers (two colors) □ blindfolds
   Activity 2
   □ coins to flip (some kids may have their own)

2. Draw a Case (Discussion) 10-15 min.
   □ pieces of paper □ pencils □ bag or box

3. A Vital Voice (Bible discussion) 10 min.
   □ Decision Making (activity piece A1 from the back of this book)

4. Now What? (Case study) 10-15 min.
   □ Decision Making (activity piece A1)

5. Finale (Prayer) 5 min.
   □ Optional: pieces of paper and pencils
   □ bag or box

BY DAVE VEERMAN

1. Making Choices

(Games) 10-15 min.

Playing a game(s) to start kids thinking about the decisions they have to make and the ways they make them. **Life is filled with decisions. Often it seems we make these decisions in the dark. Sometimes we leave them up to other people, but this can keep us from getting where we want to go. Tonight we're going to look at some of the decisions that face us in life and at some of the factors we should consider when making decisions.**

Do one (or both) of the following activities:

Activity 1 (Maze game)

Divide the group into two teams and give each team a piece of poster board, a magic marker, and a ruler. Explain that their task is to draw a maze on the poster board which a member of the other team will eventually have to navigate with a pen while blindfolded. The maze can be complicated, but it must have a clearly marked starting point and a finishing point, and the passages must be at least one inch wide. Give the teams no more than five minutes to draw their mazes.

Next have the first team choose a representative to compete. Give him/her a magic marker (different color than the one used to draw the maze), put on the blindfold, post the maze on the wall, place the marker on the starting point, and let him/her begin. The object is for the person to navigate the maze as quickly as possible with as few mistakes as possible. He or she will know which way to go by listening to the coaching of the team. Time the first team representative and then repeat the process with team number two. Add five seconds for every time the marker hits a maze wall. The winning team is the one whose representative goes through the maze the quickest. If this goes quickly, do a second round, drawing new mazes on the flip sides of the poster boards.

Following the game discuss how it relates to decision making. Address the first question to the kids who were blindfolded.

■ **In what way is the game similar to the way we sometimes go about making decisions?**

■ **Is this a good way to approach decision making? Why or why not?**

Activity 2 (Game)

Clear a large space and have the kids spread out. Make sure everyone has a coin to flip. Pick a spot in the room and tell the kids that the winner is the one who ends up closest to that spot. (You might want to give a small prize.) Explain that they can't move until you give the signal. Every

time you give the signal, they are to flip their coins. If a coin comes up heads, its owner must turn to the right and take one step forward. If the coin lands tails, its owner should turn to the left and take one step. Continue for at least ten coin flips. There will be chaos, but it will be fun and illustrate the point of how most of our unthinking decisions (those left to "chance") will end up.
- **How would you describe what happened?**
- **In what way is the game similar to the way we sometimes go about making decisions?**
- **Is this a good way to approach decision making? Why or why not?**

2. Draw a Case

(Discussion)
10-15 min.

Recognizing and discussing decisions that kids face now and will face in the future. Ask everyone to name things about which we usually must make decisions. These can include people, situations, relationships, possessions, etc. Have a volunteer write each one on separate pieces of paper and drop them into a bag or box. Get as wide a variety as possible.

Next, have the kids come up to the box one at a time, draw out a piece of paper, and describe how the item involves a decision or choice. For example, a person might draw the word "clothes," and his or her answer could be, "Every day I have to decide which clothes to wear." After everyone has had a turn, discuss the decisions that young people have to make.
- **What decisions do you make every day?**
- **What are some really life-changing decisions that you are making or will have to make soon?**
- **What factors do you consider when making decisions?**
- **What would be a good decision-making process?**

3. A Vital Choice

(Bible discussion)
10 min.

Discussing Scripture passages to discover God's role in our decision making. Hand out pencils and copies of "Decision Making" (activity piece A1 from the back of this book). Have someone read Proverbs 3:5, 6.
- **What does this say about decision making?**
(God wants to direct our paths. He must be at the center of all our decisions.)
- **How can we get God involved in our decisions?**
- **How do we trust Him with all our hearts?**
- **If we aren't supposed to lean on our own**

understanding, where does thinking come in?

(This means that we aren't supposed to be self-sufficient and lean *solely* on our ability to think and reason.)

■ **How can we acknowledge Him in all our ways?**

(We must constantly ask, "Is this what God would want?" We must also ask Him for His guidance.)

Next, have someone read Hebrews 11:6.

■ **What is faith?**

(Biblical faith includes knowledge of the facts, trust in the Person of God, and commitment/action.)

■ **How does this relate to decision making and to the Proverbs passage?**

(When we know what God wants, we must *do* it!)

Applying some decision-making steps to a case study. Point out that when kids are in high school, although they must make lots of decisions, many of their big decisions are made for them by parents, school officials, and others. Soon, however, they will have to make all their decisions themselves. In addition, point out that not choosing is really a form of choosing. Explain that not all our decisions are life changing, but there are steps to take when making important decisions. Go over the seven steps listed on the "Decision Making" sheet (activity piece A1).

Next, divide the kids into groups of three or four. Have each group read the case study and, using the seven decision-making steps, decide what Derek should do. Then have each group share its decision and how it decided.

Sharing difficult decisions and praying for God's guidance. Break into pairs and have each partner share one decision with which he or she is struggling. After both have shared, they should spend a few minutes praying for each other and for God's direction. Encourage kids to pray for their partners throughout the upcoming week. (If the group is not ready for this kind of personal sharing, close with a prayer asking for God's direction.)

Dave Veerman *is a writer for* Campus Life Leader's Guide. *Dave has more than 20 years of experience in youth ministry through* Youth for Christ, *and has written manuals for Campus Life staff members.*

□

4. Now What?

(Case study)
10-15 min.

5. Finale

(Prayer) 5 min.

Aim

Overview

You'll Need

Finding God's Will

To help young people understand how to find the will of God in their lives. Key passages: James 1:5-8 and Philippians 2:13.

Christians should desire to do what God wants at all times. Of course much of His will has been revealed in Scripture, but there are situations and decisions which are not mentioned specifically. These could involve anything from a choice of a college or career to whether or not to participate in an extracurricular activity. This meeting helps kids learn how to discover God's will in such areas. It follows naturally from the "Decisions, Decisions, Decisions" meeting in this book.

1. Searching for Answers (Game) 10-15 min.

    □ maps (one for each team)
    □ list of descriptions of the mystery place

2. Up Close and Personal (Photo identificaion) 10-15 min.

    □ ten Polaroid pictures
    □ paper and pencils
    □ prize(s)

3. Warnings (Talk) 10 min.

    □ Warnings (activity piece B1 from the back of this book) one each

4. Bible Search (Bible study) 15-20 min.

    □ Discovering God's Will (activity piece B2) one each
    □ Bibles
    □ pencils

BY DAVE VEERMAN

Playing a game that illustrates decision making. **God has revealed His will in the Bible, but this revelation does not include specific directions about many of the decisions that we face such as whether or not to go to college or who to marry. Tonight we are going to look at some of the steps involved in discovering God's will for such situations.**

Before the meeting, you should choose an obscure spot on a map and write a series of map-type descriptions of this mystery location. Here are some sample descriptions: about 65 miles from Covington, about ten minutes from a lake, near a railroad, two miles from the intersection of two state highways, 14 miles from a state park, etc.

At the meeting, have kids form teams of five to seven members each and give each team a copy of your map. Explain to the kids that each team's job is to find the mystery location by carefully following the descriptions or clues that you will give. Then read the previously written descriptions one at a time. The first team to find the exact location wins. After announcing the winner, discuss the game.

- **What was the object of this game?**
- **How does it parallel life?**

(We often need directions or clues, and our lives seem like road maps.)

Playing a game that illustrates the importance of perspective in making decisions and determining God's will for our lives. Before the meeting, use a Polaroid camera and take a color picture of ten different items. Take each picture very close to the item. Try to get the items in focus, but this is not as important as having close-up shots. Possible items could include: college catalog, wedding book, calendar, friends, church, money, etc.

At the meeting, hand out paper and pencils. Have the kids number their papers from one to ten. Next, explain that you will be passing around ten photographs (number the photographs from one to ten) which they must identify. Give them this clue: the pictures are of items that relate to their future. After all the pictures have been passed around and all the guesses made, give the answers and award a prize(s) to the kid(s) who correctly identified the most pictures.

- **Why was it difficult to identify the pictures?**
(Didn't have a good perspective, too close.)
- **How is that difficulty similar to the difficulties we face when making decisions?**

1. Searching For Answers

(Game) 10-15 min.

2. Up Close And Personal

(Photo identification) 10-15 min.

3. Warnings

(Talk) 10 min.

4. Bible Search

(Bible study)
15-20 min.

(Sometimes we can't see the answers because we are too close to the situation—we need a different perspective.)

■ **What kind of decisions do you have to make where you need help?**

■ **Where do you go to get insight and direction for your life?**

■ **Why is it important to know what God wants for your life?**

(He knows us perfectly and wants the very best for us. He has eternal perspective and sees the ultimate results of our actions. He is God, and everything we do should be pleasing to Him.)

■ **How do you find the will of God for your life?**

*R*eading some misconceptions people have about how to find the will of God. Distribute a copy of ''Warnings'' (activity piece B1 from the back of this book) to each person and talk through it.

*S*tudying the Bible to learn some practical steps to finding God's will. Distribute a copy of ''Determining God's Will'' (activity piece B2 from the back of this book) to each person. Have the kids form seven groups and assign one verse from the sheet to each group. (If the group is small, only form three or four smaller groups and assign two verses to each of them.) Have each group look up its verse and answer these questions:

■ **What does the verse say?**

■ **How does it apply to decision making?**

After about five minutes, introduce the discussion.

Are you facing a difficult decision that isn't specifically covered in Scripture (like where to go to college, how to spend your money, whether or not to take that summer trip, etc.)? Let's look at some steps that can help us be more certain of doing God's will.

Take the verses one at a time. First, have someone read the verse. Second, have group members share their answers to the questions about the verse. Third, comment briefly on each verse. You may want to use the content printed below. Encourage kids to take notes in the space provided on the Determining God's Will sheets. Be open to questions and comments as you work through each set of verses.

1. Matthew 6:33, 34

Focus on God. Seek His Kingdom. Are you willing to do what He wants no matter what it is? Ask yourself, "What is

God's will for the world?'' and ''Am I fitting in?''

2. Luke 16:10

Obey what God has already told you. Is there something that you know God wants you to do (e.g., quitting a sinful habit or forgiving your sister or brother)? Make sure you are being obedient in these known areas before you venture into the ''unknown.''

3. Philippians 4:6

Pray. Ask God to show you His will. Remember that God works through the Bible, others, and your own mind.

4. II Timothy 2:15; 3:16, 17

Study the Bible. God speaks to us through the Bible, His Holy Word. You must read it to find out what He has to say. When you read the Bible, however, look for *principles*, not specific words or proof texts. Concentrate on improving your relationship with God. Don't be like the person who reads about Paul being a tentmaker and assumes that God wants him to work for an awning company.

5. Proverbs 20:5, 18

Get counsel. Share your concerns with people who *know you* and who *know the Bible,* and ask for their advice.

6. Romans 12:2; James 1:5

Use your mind. Think. Ask for God's help and weigh all the facts. Write down your priorities, analyze your past experiences and your goals, and think through the pros and cons of the decision. And remember, God is at work within you (Phil. 2:13).

7. Luke 9:62; James 1:6-8

Act in confidence. If you have followed the six previous steps, you can make a decision, confident of God's guidance. Certainly it will be a step of faith, but that's what the Christian life is all about—walking by faith. Remember, ''Without faith it is impossible to please God'' (Heb. 11:6).

As you choose the path to take by following these seven steps, God will confirm that your choice was His as well. The process may seem long, even circuitous, but later, as you look back, you will be able to see His direct leading. Remember, God reveals His will a day at a time, a step at a time. It is up to you to take that step.

Close in prayer.

As an additional resource, you may want to recommend the InterVarsity booklet, *Affirming the Will of God*, by Paul Little.

Dave Veerman *is an experienced author and youth worker from Naperville, Illinois. Dave has written for several magazines including* Campus Life, Moody Monthly, Eternity, *and* Leadership.

□

Aim

Overview

You'll Need

Create a Date; Find a Mate

To encourage kids to explore relationship choices in their lives, especially marriage versus singleness. Key passage: I Thessalonians 4:3-8.

Kids have more control over their character development than over creating a date or finding a mate. Their most important love life needs to be with God.

1. Skin Deep (Picture show) 5-10 min.
   - □ newsprint and felt pen
   - □ photographs showing people of varying heights, weights, and physical attractiveness.

2. Create-a-Date (Work sheet) 10 min.
   - □ Create-a-Date handout (activity piece C1 from the back of this book)
   - □ colored pencils or pens
   - □ scissors and tape

3. Advertise Yourself (Bible study) 15-20 min.
   - □ The Personals (activity piece C2)
   - □ chalkboard and chalk
   - □ Bibles

4. Issues and answers (Panel discussion) 15-20 min.
   - □ 3'' x 5'' cards and pens
   - □ newsprint and felt pen
   - □ Bibles

BY SUE TOMAN

Examining our prejudices about people's looks. Display photographs of various people (male and female, young and old, short and tall, attractive and not so attractive, etc.). Have kids say what their first impressions of each picture are. Encourage them to say immediately what comes to mind. Give your honest impressions if needed to help break the ice, or if you sense the group is being too nice to be real. As people comment, write the gist of their thoughts on a piece of paper. After they finish commenting, attach that picture to the piece of paper. Have them comment on all the pictures.

Next, have kids look a second time at each picture. Tell them to imagine they are the person in the picture.

☐ **Do you think you would like to be this person? Why or why not?**

☐ **How do you think you might feel about yourself if you were this person?**

You know the old saying, "Beauty is only skin deep," and yet we often judge others only on that basis, especially when it comes to dating. Certainly, in choosing dates and eventually a mate, we have to make judgments. But Jesus says, "Stop judging by mere appearances, and make a right judgment" (Jn. 7:24, NIV). This meeting is going to be about making those right judgments in every area of the dating and marriage question.

Examining our tastes and values in the opposite sex. **Although we put far too much emphasis on outward appearance, nobody considers only another person's looks. We also have preferences in terms of personality, interests, and life-style. This is only natural and good. But we can get in trouble here, too.**

Hand out the "Create-a-Date" work sheet (activity piece C1 from the back of this book).

Give kids scissors, tape, and colored pens and let them create their ideal dates from the options on the handout. When they have finished, have them share their composite pictures and get a few laughs.

☐ **This was just for fun, but if you could actually choose your ideal mate, what qualities would you look for?**

☐ **If you had to sacrifice some qualities, which would you be willing to let go of and which would you keep? Why?**

☐ **If you could come up with a simple moral about**

1. Skin Deep

(Picture show) 5-10 min.

2. Create-a-Date

(Work sheet) 10 min.

beauty or the lack of it, what would it be?
Here are some examples to share:
1. Beauty is temporary. Normally, with age, it lessens.
2. Beauty is a gift, not something earned.
3. Beauty is fragile. It can be destroyed in a fire, a car accident, through illness.
4. Learn to see beauty wholistically. In other words, learn to honestly regard people as attractive not only for looks, but also for aspects of their character such as kindness, sense of humor, loyalty.

---

3. Advertise Yourself

(Bible study) 15-20 min.

Examining the qualities we'd like to be judged by and the qualities God wants us to have. Hand out "The Personals" (activity piece C2) and have kids read the ads. Ask them what these people seem to be looking for, writing down responses on a chalkboard (for example: sex, intelligence, wealth). Ask kids to add to the list any other things they think people *should* look for in someone they date.

Look at each thing they listed as a group. Ask whether they would like or not like being evaluated on that criteria and why or why not. Ask kids if any of the criteria seem unfair to use in evaluating someone. Have them list the items in order of their importance.

■ **Are any of the items essential, such as "that the person be a Christian"? Why or why not?**

The next activity looks at what God values in people. What He values is what we should strive to be. As we do, we will become better prospective mates and also be more prepared to be what God intends—the Bride of Christ.

Have kids create their own ad after looking up the following verses: I Peter 3:3, 4; I Thessalonians 4:3-8; and Galatians 5:13-26. Have them note characteristics God values and detests and work them into their ads as appropriate. After a few kids share their ads, remind them we need to seek others who are striving to be godly, but we can't expect to find a perfect person.

---

4. Issues And Answers

(Panel discussion) 15-20 min.

Raising the tough questions about singleness, dating, and marriage. One way to deal with the questions raised in a meeting like this is to wrap it up with a panel of "experts"—both kids and adults. Here are two issues you should raise if they don't come up:

Meeting C

■ **Which is better, singleness or marriage? What are the benefits and drawbacks of both singleness and marriage?**

You can point out that the vast majority of people spend a portion of their adult lives in singleness and a portion in marriage. Both marriage and singleness can be gifts from God. It is important to learn to accept the gift given to you. It can be hard to believe, but God always gives you what is best for you at the time. Not necessarily in terms of what you want most, but in terms of what will cause you to grow more Christlike.

■ **How many kids actually date during high school? What is the correlation between dating habits and marriage?**

Take a secret poll and find out how many of your kids actually date. You—and they—may be surprised at how small the percentage is. Even if most of your kids do date, those who don't need to know that that's okay. Point out also that the choices kids make in the kind of people they date during high school (and especially the kind of physical involvement they get into) often influence the choices they make in the kind of people they marry.

Whether you date or not, you do make choices about the kind of people you hang around with. And chances are, the person you marry will be like those people. You need to think about whether that's the type of person you really want.

Close in directed silent prayer. First, have kids tell God they love Him and why. Remind them how much we enjoy having someone to love us and tell us how wonderful we are. Have kids admit their desire for that special person to God. Then have them confess any times they have judged the opposite sex by unfair criteria. Finally, have kids pray that God would make them fit to be the Bride of Christ. And thank Him for His promise to meet *all* of our needs.

Sue Toman is a probation officer with the Circuit Court of Michigan. She worked with college students on InterVarsity staff for four years and has also been a counselor in a youth home. Sue has contributed a number of articles on discipleship, singleness, and dating to HIS magazine. She lives in Grand Rapids, Michigan.

Aim

Overview

You'll Need

Keep Up The Good Work!

To help kids see that work is from God and that they can begin preparing for a meaningful career by being good stewards of what God has already given them. Key Passage: Matthew 25:14-30.

Lots of people don't like work. This is especially true of senior highs who often work in rather meaningless jobs. Today's session will help kids see that work can be a good thing and that their current and near-future jobs can help prepare them for rewarding lifelong careers.

1. What's My Line? (Game) 5 min.
   □ paper and pencils

2. It's a Living (Discussion) 10-15 min.
   □ chalkboard or newsprint
   □ Bibles

3. It Takes Talents (Bible study) 15-20 min.
   □ Bibles

4. Working It Out (Self-Assessment) 15-20 min.
   □ Who, Me? (activity piece D1 from the back of this book)
   □ pencils

BY RICK & ELLEN THOMPSON

*T*hinking about work by asking questions to guess the occupation of a "mystery guest." Choose one kid to be the mystery guest. Secretly tell him or her what his or her occupation is. Other kids will then take turns asking yes or no questions to try and determine what the occupation is. Keep track of the number of questions. After ten questions, have kids write down on pieces of paper what they think the occupation is. Have them share their guesses. Play again if time permits.

You may be wondering why we played this little game. Today we're going to be talking about work. It's something all of us have to do at some time or other (like every day!). So let's see how we can make the best of it.

---

*U*nderstanding that work is a gift from God, even though it can be abused.
■ **Let's start by listing all the words that come to your mind that describe work.**
List their descriptions on the board. Then lead your kids in a *brief* discussion about the good and bad side of work using Scripture as a discussion starter. Here is an outline to guide your discussion. Pick and choose what you would like to bring out:

1. Work itself is good.
God Himself is a God of work (Gen. 2:2; Eph. 2:10).
Jesus worked (Jn. 5:17).
God ordained work before sin entered the world (Gen. 1:28; 2:15).
God commands us to work and to rest (Ex. 34:21).
We should enjoy our work (Eccl. 3:22).
Not working is bad (Prov. 10:26; 12:24; 14:23; 15:19; 19:15; 21:25).
Work is necessary to buy food (II Thess. 3:10)
Work also builds character and adds to our self-esteem

2. Because of sin, work can be bad.
Work can be painful and difficult (Gen. 3:17-19).
Some work can be tedious.
Some work is dangerous.
It is possible to like work too much (workaholism).

So it looks like, on the whole, work is a good thing.

1. What's My Line?
(Game) 5-10 min.

2. It's A Living
(Discussion)
10-15 min.

3. It Takes Talent

(Bible study)
15-20 min.

But what about a job at a fast-food joint or something like that? Can that be good for anything more than money? Jesus told a parable that has something to say about this.

*S*eeing that God expects us to be good stewards of the gifts He has given us. Read the Parable of the Talents, Matthew 25:14-30, which shows us how to live while Jesus is away.

■ **What's the point of this parable? Why do you suppose the third servant didn't put his talent to use? When are we like that man?**

Give your students some time to discuss these questions. Work on making the parable relevant to them. Get them to see that no matter how much we start with, God expects the same: He expects us to be good and faithful servants using the gifts He has given. The reward for our faithfulness is even greater responsibility and the joy that comes only through obedience.

■ **What does this parable say about jobs?**

Kids may have some difficulty making a connection here. Through your leading, they can see that their current jobs, no matter how dull or routine, are from God, and our investment in those jobs can have a real payoff. Hard work will be rewarded, perhaps not in the current job, but in a future job. Building positive and loving relationships with coworkers and supervisors will also bring rewards. Share other examples of this principle with them.

Now we're all going to get a chance to see how this parable applies to us today. Let's take a look at the talents we have been given.

4. Working It Out

(Self-assessment)
15-20 min.

*L*isting God-given talents and thinking about ways to develop the ones in which future employers will be most interested. Pass out one copy of the "Who, Me?" work sheet (activity piece D1 from the back of this book) to each student. Have kids fill out section one (listing of skills, abilities, resources). Share lists with the rest of the group if time permits and if students have developed an adequate level of trust in each other to share something so personal. You be the judge of that!

Next have them complete section two of the work sheet. In this section students are to rank the abilities in the order that they think are most important. Tell them that actual employers also ranked these abilities. After kids are all done, tell them how employers ranked them. Have them write the employer rankings next to their own as you read them.

Attribute/Employer Ranking

Oral communication/1

Motivation/2

Initiative/3

Assertiveness/4

Loyalty/5

Leadership/6

Maturity/7

Enthusiasm/8

Punctuality/9

Appearance/10

Written communication/11

Work experience/12

Grades/13

Disposition/14

Extroversion/15

From "The Christian Job Hunter," by Pamela J. Moran (Ann Arbor, Michigan: Servant Books, 1984), p. 139. The list in this helpful book contains 26 attributes, the top 15 of which are shown above. The survey was conducted only among employers in the business field. The list would probably vary depending on the occupation.

■ **How does your list compare to that of the employers?**

This session has only scratched the surface of the topic of job hunting. You can explore this topic further by reading books like the one above, or *What Color Is Your Parachute?* Revised edition by Richard N. Bolles (Ten Speed Press, 1981). If you want to expand this topic into a month-long study, a good course on the subject is "Decisions! Decisions!—Matching Personal Potential with Career Options," a *Christian Growth Electives* course from David C. Cook Publishing Co.

Conclude today's session by calling attention to the few words of advice printed at the bottom of the "Who, Me?" sheet. Encourage kids to ask further questions or make comments about jobs and work. Make sure they realize that there are steps they can be taking now to prepare themselves for their careers.

Close the session in prayer, thanking God for work and for the abilities He has given each of us. Ask Him to help us be responsible stewards in our work.

Rick Thompson is a research manager. He teaches management courses at Judson College, Elgin, Illinois. He also teaches Sunday school and has written another meeting in the Pacesetter series. Ellen Thompson is Director of the Career Center and Christian Ministries at Judson College. She is a former staff worker with InterVarsity. Rick and Ellen live in Elgin, Illinois.

□

Aim

Overview

You'll Need

What's Money For?

To help kids gain a Biblical perspective on money and possessions. Key passage: Ecclesiastes 5:10-20.

Money is a gift from God meant to be used wisely like all His other gifts, but it becomes a cruel and deceptive idol when it is made an end in itself. Regardless of kids' financial status, they must decide what priority they will place on material wealth and what use they will make of it. This meeting helps kids develop a Biblical attitude toward money and begin to decide how they will use it.

1. What Do You Want? (Survey) 10-15 min.
   ☐ What Do You Want Out of Life? (activity piece E1 from the back of this book) one each
   ☐ pencils

2. What's Money For? (Bible study) 15-20 min.
   ☐ What's Money For? (activity piece E2 from the back of this book) one each
   ☐ Bibles
   ☐ pencils

3. Fate of a $20 Bill (Debate) 15-20 min.
   ☐ $20 bill
   ☐ watch
   ☐ paper
   ☐ pencils

4. Commit What You Have (Decision) 5 min.

BY SANDY LARSEN

Meeting E

*C*ompleting a survey to help kids see their attitudes toward material things. Hand out pencils and copies of "What Do You Want Out of Life?" (activity piece E1 from the back of this book). Give kids eight minutes for completing the survey. At the end of that time, ask for some sample responses to the questions. At this point, do not challenge answers or point out mistakes. The purpose of the survey is simply to help teens see their own attitudes toward material wealth. But do make note of students' conflicting answers, which show how differing values affect people's attitudes toward material things.

Some people think the Bible says that "money is the root of all evil." Look at I Timothy 6:10 to see how the quote actually goes.

Have someone read the verse out loud. Point out that it is the *love* of money that is condemned.

It's an important difference because it's our attitude, even more than the money itself, that's important. We must decide what we'll do with the material things God gives us.

*S*tudying a passage of Scripture to discover God's perspective on money. Have kids form groups of three or four and then distribute the Bible study sheet "What's Money For?" (activity piece E2 from the back of this book). Make sure enough Bibles are available for all students. Tell them:

This Bible study contains six false statements. By reading Ecclesiastes 5:10-20 you'll find the six corresponding true statements. Follow the directions on your study sheet.

As groups work, offer help to any who have questions. After about ten minutes, have groups share their answers and explain them. Use the material below to guide their understanding of the passages.

1. vs. 15. You can't take it with you, and money will not buy a person eternal life either. (Of course, some people use this truth as an excuse to live it up in this life, as Paul quoted in I Corinthians 15:32.)

2. vs. 19. It's good to enjoy God's gifts which are legitimately given in His will, so long as the gifts themselves are not elevated to the status of a god.

3. vs. 10. If you love money, you always want more. (That's the "root of all evil" and the evil here is covetousness. Our advertising-soaked culture won't leave our

1. What Do You Want?

(Survey) 10-15 min.

2. What's Money For?

(Bible study)
15-20 min.

desires in peace, but constantly tells us we have to have more.)

4. vs. 12. Having a lot of goods means worrying about losing them. The more valuable they are to us, the more worried we'll be about their loss.

5. vss. 13, 14. All kinds of things can happen to our possessions and our investments.

6. vs. 18. Work can be enjoyed. God made people to work. In fact, it is God who enables people to enjoy their work.

Next, discuss the two general conclusions at the end of the sheet. Point out two possible (but by no means final) conclusions that can be drawn from Ecclesiastes 5:10-20:

1. Money/possessions can give you temporary pleasure and an appreciation for God's generosity.

2. Money/possessions cannot give you ultimate joy or eternal life, or even true security in this life.

Money is a good gift from God. It can be misused as well as used as He wants it to be. We all come from different kinds of financial situations. But we're all in the same boat because we all have to decide what to do with what we have, and how important it will be to us to accumulate more.

3. Fate of a $20 Bill

(Debate) 15-20 min.

*C*omparing the different uses of money that result from Christian and unchristian values. Show your group a $20 bill and ask for some suggestions of how to use it. (Answers will probably range from "Give it to me!" to "Take us all out for pizza after the meeting!") Tell the group you're sure they can come up with many more possible uses for this $20 bill.

Divide the group into two teams, the C-Team and the D-Team. Tell the C-Team that they stand for Christ's use of money and the D-Team that they stand for the Devil's use of money.

Write down all the uses you can think of for this $20 bill, based on Christ's values or the Devil's values for money. Then select two representatives for your team. You will be having a debate between Christ's team and the Devil's team for how this money should be used. Here's how the debate will work:

D-Team presentation of case—Speaker 1 (3 min.)
C-Team presentation of case—Speaker 1 (3 min.)
D-Team rebuttal—Speaker 2 (2 min.)
C-Team rebuttal—Speaker 2 (2 min.)

I will be the judge of which team has presented the better case for how the $20 should be used. Before we begin, though, I should tell you that the $20 bill is still mine and only I will decide how it will really be used!

When the debate is over, congratulate both teams and point out convincing points that each made. Pick the winning team based on which one presented the strongest case, regardless of the values they based their case on. (If the Devil's team won, have the group discuss what points Christ's team could have used to strengthen its argument.)

■ **What values did the D-Team have that gave rise to their rotten suggestions about how to use my money?**

(Selfish, dethroning God, worldly, foolish, pleasure centered, temporary rather than eternal.)

■ **What values did the C-Team have that prompted their beautiful suggestions for the fate of my $20?**

(God centered, meeting honest obligations, helping others, eternal values, unselfish, pure, honoring God.)

■ **Were some suggestions on both lists? If so, why?**

(Sometimes our needs and the needs of those around us determine good and bad uses of money.)

If time and your finances allow, announce that you will treat your group to something special like pizza or ice cream.

***

Deciding to use a particular amount of money or a resource for God. Emphasize that each of us has a choice about our values, and our values will demonstrate themselves in how we use our money and other material possessions money can buy. **Let's pray that God will help us decide to use what we own for Him. We may have to start small, but that's the best way to form new habits in our use of money.**

Lead the group in a time of silent prayer in which each member privately confesses a poor use of money and before God commits himself or herself to a specific act of service through money. (You will want to participate also.) Allow a few minutes at each step.

Finally, close the meeting by praying aloud. Thank God for His many good gifts and ask for His help to have His values about them.

Sandy Larsen is a free-lance writer in Ashland, Wisconsin. In the past, she has worked with both senior and junior high youth in churches, camps, and street evangelism. Her publications include several Bible study books for youth.

4. Commit What You Have

(Decision) 5 min.

1

The Great Debate

Ask two interested teens or teams of students to debate an age-old question: "Is following God's will more like using a blueprint, or making your own decisions based on broad, Biblical principles?" Make available books and articles on the topic (look in Christian bookstores and libraries). Also encourage each side to interview church leaders for points to emphasize.

You might advertise in the church bulletin for help from a debating coach. Be sure to allot time for presentation, rebuttal, and final comments.

2

The Great Paper Caper

Making major life decisions requires strategies, not blind groping. In advance, buy two (or more) packages of notebook paper, the bigger the better. Remove ten or so sheets from each (so the number of sheets will be different from what the package says); be sure both have the same number of sheets.

Divide kids into two teams (or teams of four or five kids each). Explain that the object is to find the number of sheets in the team's stack in the shortest amount of time—without crumpling any of the paper. Encourage kids to use a strategy to accomplish the goal. Give teams a few minutes to plan and then shout "Go!"

Name the first team to correctly count its stack the "Paper Caper Champs." Ask them what strategy they used to count the pages. Ask the same question of the losers. Then explain that when we tackle a big project, it usually pays to have a strategy, a plan. Otherwise, we waste time and energy. Some people make major decisions without a strategy. What strategies do your teens use? Are they good ones?

BY LUCY TOWNSEND

3

Life's Tough Choices

Use a survey to get an idea of what decisions your teens are grappling with and how they feel about their decision-making ability. Below are some sample questions:
1. Name two or more big decisions you must make in the next few years.
2. Which decisions seem the toughest to make?
3 What big decisions have you made within the last year?
4. What steps did you take to make those decisions?
5. Do you feel you usually know how to make decisions?
6. What more would you like to know about decision making?

4

Life Map

Have kids write a life map. Ask them to jot down three activities that have given them the greatest enjoyment. These can be hobbies, sports, church work, school projects, etc. Then have them recall several projects they completed which gave them the greatest sense of accomplishment. Provide kids with a list of jobs (from the public library). Have them find jobs that are similar to the activities they have enjoyed most. Explain that often an adult realizes later in life that he began to cultivate an area of expertise in early childhood. For example, an interior designer remembered that she had enjoyed decorating paper houses before she was ten years old.

5

Thumbs Up, Thumbs Down

To help teens discover their career interests, have them list three or four jobs they'd really love, and three or four they'd really hate. Then have them think about specific factors that contribute to their opinions. For example, they may hate to collect garbage because the work is done outdoors, even in sub-zero weather; it is smelly; it can be dangerous; and it involves little creativity or intellectual challenge. By thinking specifically about different occupations, teens can discover what they value. After listing positive and negative factors, have them rank them in order of importance. For example, working outside in cold weather may not be really important, but lack of creativity may be very important. After teens have listed these factors, list them on the chalkboard and discuss.

Illustration by Donna Nelson

6

Volunteer Search

One of the best ways to discover whether an occupation would appeal to a particular person is for him or her to do some volunteer work in that field. For example, an aspiring nurse might work as a candy striper. An aspiring lawyer might work in a law office. Assign teams to call up businesses and institutions (hospitals, law firms, schools) to see if volunteer workers are welcome. Have teams report their findings to the group.

8

Mind Your Money

The youth programs of many churches have budgets. Find out what your budget is (if you do not already know), and share that information with teens. If figures are available, show them how their budget was spent the previous year. You might also show them what proportion of the total church budget is spent directly by and for them. Divide teens into groups, and ask them to evaluate the budget.

- Has the money been spent wisely?
- Can costs be cut anywhere?
- If teens controlled the budget, how would they spend the money this year?
- What items (other things) do they need that are not covered by the budget?
- How might they raise money for an important item not covered in the budget?

Have each group report its findings.

7

College . . . ?

Some teens in your youth group may be seriously questioning whether they should go to college after high school. Why not have a panel discussion in which several adults who are pleased with their careers discuss what they did after high school? The choice of guests is important. Try to have a mixture—those who went directly to college, those who began their careers immediately, and those who entered college several years later. Discuss with this group the pros and cons of their decisions, etc. Some panelists might prefer receiving written questions before coming to the session.

9

College for A Day

Why not take a carload of kids on a tour of several local colleges? The trip will be even more enjoyable if former youth group members meet kids at the college and show them around. Depending on the interests of your group, include a variety of schools: a community college, a liberal arts college, Bible college, university, technical institute, etc. Kids will enjoy the trip even more if you take them to your alma mater.

11

Magazine Mystique

Have teens bring either a magazine they love or hate to a meeting and be ready to discuss the following:

- Who is the publication trying to reach (age, income, specific interests)?
- What are most of the articles about?
- What are the advertisements like?
- What probably appeals to people who buy the publication?

Have volunteers show their magazines and discuss these issues. Then have the group decide what values are conveyed by these publications. If, for example, the magazine has beautiful models and expensive clothing, perhaps beauty and wealth are the important values. If it contains many articles about electric guitars and music, it conveys the impression that music is important. How do these values relate to Scripture?

10

Values Pies

With markers, have teens draw two pies. The first should show what part of their week is designated for studies, sleep, family chores, work, church, dating, athletics, etc. The second pie should show what the pie would look like if teens could control all of their time. For example, if someone hates school and loves to practice basketball, he might substitute basketball for school. Or he might simply cut down on the hours he spends in one activity. Have kids share their pies with each other. Share your own pies and explain that our ideal pie shows what we value. How much of our week do we spend thinking about and getting to know God?

12

Tape and Tacos

Direct an interview team to arrange and tape sessions with several parents and other church members. Focus the session on one critical decision that the person had to make and the part God played in that decision. How did each person know that God was leading him or her? How often did he or she ask for His guidance? What were the options and how did each person finally make a decision? Did the person question himself or herself after he or she made the decision? If so, how did the person resolve those questions? Have kids listen to the tapes at a taco feast.

14

The Expert Says . . .

Visit the church library, local library, and Christian bookstores. Look for books and magazine articles on making career choices, selecting a college, deciding on a marriage partner, and managing money. Have kids check out or buy books or magazines that interest them and report on their reading at the next several meetings.

13

The Job Doctor

Do your teens know that most people lose or change their jobs because of interpersonal conflicts? Divide teens into small groups and allow them ten minutes to practice roleplaying difficult job-related situations. For example, a boss might constantly criticize the teen's work, a co-worker might refuse to do his share, etc. After each roleplay, have teens assume the role of job doctor who recommends strategies for dealing with these hassles.

15

My One And Only

Divide teens into small groups and have them brainstorm what they look for in a person they'd date. Afterwards, list items on the board and have teens number the top ten qualities on their own papers. See what items are important to most kids. How do teens' lists compare with their leaders'? With those of a marriage counselor? (See the activity, "Throw Advice Before Rice.")

16

Consummate Cooks

Can your teens plan and prepare a meal on a tight budget? Divide the group into teams, and see how they fare preparing a meal for themselves. Budget each team $1.50 a person. Teams must plan a menu, go to the grocery store, prepare food, and serve it at the next meeting. Appoint an inspector (perhaps an adult sponsor) who evaluates the cost of the meal, its nutritional value, its taste, etc., and declares the winners "Consummate Cooks."

18

Throw Advice Before Rice

Invite a Christian marriage counselor to be a guest speaker. Beforehand, discuss with this person some things that teens should know before taking the wedding vows. What are some typical problems that emerge after the couple has been married? How does a teen know what kind of mate to look for? Are there some steps a teen can take to prepare for marriage before actually meeting a possible mate? Suggest that teens write some questions in advance of the counselor's visit.

17

Is the Price Right?

Are your teens ready for the demands of marriage or living away from home? You can help them find out by pairing them up and having them total costs for the following items:

- Average monthly rent for an apartment in the area;
- Monthly payments on an inexpensive car;
- Monthly payment for health insurance;
- Average monthly gas, water, and light payment for an apartment;
- Typical monthly grocery bill for two single people/married couple;

19

Decisions, Decisions

Announce in your church bulletin and newsletter that your students would like to hear what individuals have learned from making decisions about singleness and marriage. Interested persons might write anonymous histories and mail them to the church office by a certain date. Be sure to encourage parents to submit their histories. Invite both teens and their parents to a session in which histories are read and discussed. Do any teens recognize their parents' stories?

Dr. Lucy F. Townsend *is a freelance writer, teacher, and editor from Elgin, Illinois. Lucy has written or edited hundreds of articles and curriculum pieces, and contributed four courses to the award-winning* Young Teen Action *for junior high youth groups (Cook).*

Dealing With CONFLICT

A look at
how conflicts arise and how groups
can solve them.

BY GARY W. DOWNING

Wherever two or three are gathered together . . . you're sure to have a fight! Doesn't that seem to be the way things go? You tried so hard to build unity; you meant well; but now you're faced with conflict in your group. What can you do?

Understanding Conflict

In order to deal with conflict it is necessary to understand how it arises. Conflict usually occurs when two ingredients vital to a group's health are missing or break down. The most important element for a healthy group is *communication.* Effective communication occurs only when a message is received, understood, and responded to. Part of good communication is listening "in stereo," listening both to facts and feelings, and to information and emotions.

Commitment is another key element for a healthy group. Unclear commitments result in imbalanced relationships which lead to frustration, fear, and anger. Setting standards for involvement and behavior is one way of helping people express their commitment to a group and thus avoiding imbalanced relationships.

The best way to deal with conflict is to avoid it altogether by developing communication and commitment. But having said that, even the best led groups will experience conflict.

How can you redirect conflict in such a way that communication and commitment are actually enhanced through the painful process?

A Win-Win Situation

First, work at avoiding a win-lose outcome. People approach conflict differently. Some avoid it at all costs. They would rather lose than fight. Others attack aggressively because they feel that winning is everything. Still others seek a compromise or an accommodation so that neither side loses, but neither wins.

These approaches will only result in more conflict later. You need to develop the possibility of a win-win outcome by employing these practical principles:

Face the conflict! Name it and encourage everyone involved to stick with the problem and to resolve it peacefully. Use statements like: "I sense we have to stop and work on a problem." "I feel uncomfortable, because you two aren't seeing eye to eye." Conflict is as obvious as a wart on your nose. Avoiding it doesn't do any good, but separating the opposing parties can be a very positive move if it allows you to proceed to the next phase.

Clarify the problems. What is really causing the hurt or anger or fear? What assumptions are being made that may not be accurate? What does each party in the conflict really want? What specific behavior is causing the negative feelings? How do the participants in the conflict feel at that moment?

Getting the problem on the table makes it more possible to deal with it honestly and openly.

Look for alternatives. What would each party like to see happen? What are some specific changes each wants to make? What might the participants be willing to do differently in the future? How can they work together to solve the problem instead of dividing the group?

Move towards reconciliation. Ask the contending parties questions like these: "What part of the problem are you willing to confess to and ask forgiveness for?" "Are you willing to actually forgive the other party who has hurt you?" "Are you able to respect the opposition enough to insist that everyone involved have a chance to speak, and to listen seriously?" "Will you commit yourself to working through alternatives so that all can feel better about themselves?"

The Biblical Model

———————■———————

When conflicts arise, follow the Biblical "formula" in Matthew 18. (If I have an offense with another Christian, I go to him or her first. If I cannot resolve the offense, I bring another Christian friend along as a reconciling witness. If we still cannot achieve reconciliation, then we take it to the larger group for it to resolve.) I must be willing to acknowledge that the relationship is more important than whether I win or lose the argument.

Conflict is inevitable, but reconciliation is always possible by God's grace. Communication and commitment are possible in spite of natural human differences because of Christ's healing presence in our lives. Claim that power and become a reconciling friend maker and peacemaker in your group.

Practice Activity

———————■———————

It is both helpful and fun for a group to practice sharing negative feelings. Family communication theory offers some good models for developing interactive skills. Here are some common principles:

A. Use "I" statements—don't talk about someone else's feelings; take the risk of sharing your own. Examples: "Here's how I feel." "Right or wrong, this is where I am right now."

B. Talk directly to the person toward whom you have negative feelings. Look your antagonist in the eyes and try to convey why you are hurt, angry, or fearful. Be honest, forthright, and specific about your negative feelings.

C. Be specific about behavior that is causing you pain or discomfort. Deal with the conflict right away, but have a goal of reconciliation, not intimidation.

D. Offer acceptable, alternative behavior in the form of a wish—not a coercive demand. If the other party refuses to respond, communicate your feelings about his or her rejection or

denial of your offer. Keep responding and attempting to communicate until you either lose energy or the heart to continue.

As an exercise, have kids form pairs and role play sharing negative feelings with their partners. Use this formula:

"When you did this . . . (talk about specific behavior), I felt this way . . . (share a feeling), and I wish you would do this instead . . . (offer an alternative)."

Give your group members a contrived situation to practice. For example, have them enact the exchange between a mom who feels like her son doesn't take her seriously when he refuses to take out the garbage.

Then, suggest they roleplay an actual experience or conflict they had recently. Have members respond as naturally as possible to their partners, sometimes accepting and other times rejecting their offer of self-disclosure. Discuss the results.

In addition to practicing communication, your group might find it helpful to establish some ground rules for participation and some guidelines for behavior. Keep them short and realistic. After discussing them, an agreement can be written up and even signed by those who choose to participate. □

Dr. Gary W. Downing *is executive minister of the Colonial Church of Edina, Minnesota. Formerly he was executive director for Youth Leadership and was part of the National Training Staff for Young Life.*

BY DALE VONSEGGEN

My Choices . . . Which Voices?

A P u p p e t S c r i p t

Characters

■

"Cautious" Carl: Has a great deal of trouble making decisions. Carl tends to do nothing because he can't decide what to do.

"Random" Randy: Makes quick random decisions based on chance or whim.

"Conditional" Carmen: Makes decisions based on fleeces, and places conditions on every decision.

"Worldly" Wally: Makes his choices based only on human, selfish motivations.

Pastor Wayne: Helps Carl learn how to make good decisions.

Scene 1

■

Carl and Randy are seated in a pizza parlor.

RANDY: Carl, old buddy, I never see you going out with any girls. You're a pretty sharp guy. What's the problem?

CARL: Well, I just can't decide who to ask out. About the time I get my courage up, I change my mind and want to ask someone else.

RANDY: So you never get around to asking *anyone* out. That's really too bad.

CARL: How do *you* decide who to ask out?

RANDY: Oh, no problem. I just pick one that looks good, and ZAP!!! I ask her out. Once I even decided, "I'm going to ask out the fifth girl that walks through that door."

CARL: And what happened?

RANDY: I counted the girls as they came in, and when the fifth one came through the door, I asked her out.

CARL: Was she a real winner?

RANDY: Wellll . . . not really. I found out that she had a "wait" problem.

CARL: Uh oh. A real BIG one, huh?

RANDY: No, but when I went to pick her up, I had to *wait* on her for two hours!

CARL: Hmmm. Any other suggestions?

RANDY: Sometimes I open the yearbook with my eyes closed, point to a page, and then ask out whoever I'm pointing to.

CARL: Sounds pretty dangerous to me. Hey! We'd better decide what kind of pizza we want. *(Looking at menu)* Let's get sausage and mushroom . . . no, let's get pepperoni. Or how about onions and green peppers?

RANDY *(Impatiently)*: Here, let me use my method of making decisions. Carl, Carl, you're too slow, catch a pizza by its dough *(Pointing to menu)*. There! We'll order *that* one. *(Carl looks closely at the menu.)*

CARL: Bacon, Pineapple, and anchovies? I don't think I'm very hungry.

RANDY: Aw, come on. You might like it!

CARL: Naw, I gotta go. I need to meet with Pastor Wayne tonight. He's going to help me with some decisions I have to make.

RANDY: Come on—you don't have to go to Pastor Wayne for help. Let old Randy give you a hand. I use the "Pop it, pick it, and prove it" system to find helpful Bible verses.

CARL: "Pop it, pick it, and prove it?"

RANDY: Just pop open your Bible at random, pick out a verse, and trust God to make it happen. Works every time. Do you have your Bible here?

CARL: Sure. I have it here in my backpack. *(Finds it)* Here it is. *(Hands it to Randy)*

RANDY: Now watch. Just hold the Bible, close your eyes, pop the Bible open, pick a verse . . . .

CARL *(very attentively)*: What's the verse?

RANDY: It's Psalm 50:13. "Do I eat the flesh of bulls, or drink the blood of goats?"

CARL *(Turning away, covering his mouth)*: Uh . . . I don't feel hungry at all. I really do need to get going. I'm not sure your method works so well. *(Exiting)* I'll see you later.

RANDY: You know, I'm not very hungry either. I think I'll go, too. *(Exits)*

Scene 2

Carmen is at her locker. Carl enters and approaches her hesitantly.

CARL: Uh . . . Carmen . . . do you think . . . I mean . . . would you like to . . . uh . . . you wouldn't want to go with me to the game Saturday night, would you?

CARMEN: Well, *if* it doesn't rain, and *if* I'm feeling okay, and *if* no one else asks me, yes, I'll go with you. *(Pause)* That is, *if* I don't have to work at the truck stop Saturday night.

CARL: You're working at the truck stop? What doing?

CARMEN: I got a job as a waitress. I decided not to go to college.

CARL: What made you decide that?

CARMEN: I learned a new way to make decisions at our Bible study last week.

CARL: What is it? Maybe it would work for me, too. I've been having a hard time making some of my decisions.

CARMEN: What kind of decisions?

CARL: Like what courses to take next term, or whether to buy a car or not, or what girl to ask out.

CARMEN: Oh, no problem. My system really works.

CARL: Tell me about it.

CARMEN: Well, it's found in Judges chapter 6. It's using "fleeces."

CARL: Fleeces? What are fleeces?

CARMEN: Gideon used fleeces, which were skins of sheep, to help him know for sure that God was going to use him to save Israel. Gideon asked God to give him a physical sign, so he would know for sure that he was doing the right thing. So now, that's how I do it.

CARL: Give me an example.

CARMEN: I told God that *if* He wanted me to go to college, that He should help me get the Wellbright Scholarship—you know—the one that pays for everything. That was my fleece for God.

CARL: And what happened?

CARMEN: I didn't get the scholarship. So that made it perfectly clear to me that God didn't want me to go to college.

CARL: Sounds simple. And what about the truck stop job?

CARMEN: I told God that *if* He wanted me to take a job, that He should show me what job to take—you know—give me a "sign."

CARL: And?

CARMEN: And last Saturday night we stopped at the truck stop for a sandwich, and there was my "sign," as plain as day: "HELP WANTED." So I asked about the job, and they hired me!

CARL: And you think that's God's plan for your life?

CARMEN: Of course! I asked, and He answered! And He answered fast!!

CARL: I guess so. Well, if I don't see you Saturday night, at least I'll see you Sunday in church.

CARMEN: Oh, no. I have to work *every Sunday* from 8:00 a.m. to 8:00 p.m. So I won't be going to church for a while.

CARL: That's too bad. Well, I sure wish I knew what God's plan for my life is. I'm so mixed up, I don't know what to do.

CARMEN *(As they exit)*: Now, *if* God wants you to find a neat girl friend, first you need a sharp car. So *if* you see a sharp car for sale, you need to buy it—no matter what!

Scene 3

———————————— ■ ————————————

Carl is pacing back and forth, troubled.

CARL: Boy, I sure wish I knew what classes to take next term. And what God wants me to do with my life. Maybe I should "pop" my Bible open, and . . . no . . . maybe I should try one of those fleeces Carmen was talking about. Now *if* God wants me to be a preacher, I need to . . . to learn how to yell and pound on the pulpit. No . . . that doesn't make any sense. *(Wally enters)*

WALLY: Hey, pal! You look troubled. What's bothering you?

CARL: Well, I have some big decisions to make, and . . . and I'm having trouble.

WALLY: What kind of decisions?

CARL: Oh, decisions like what courses to take, and what career I should go into.

WALLY: Let me help you. To decide what classes to take, talk to someone who took the courses last year. Then sign up for the classes that require the least amount of work.

CARL: How is that God's plan? I don't get it.

WALLY: God wants you to get your rest, right? And you need time to go to church, to read your Bible, and to do lots of other things for Him. He certainly doesn't want you to waste all your time doing homework!

CARL: What about selecting an occupation? How did you do that?

WALLY: Easy. I went to the library and did some research on what kind of jobs pay the most money for the least amount of work.

CARL: And did you find out?

WALLY: Well, professional athletes and rock singers were way up there. And since I'm not much of an athlete, I decided to become a rock singer. Would you like to try out for my band? I'm going to call it *Smash!*

CARL: No, I think I'll pass. That's not the kind of job I want to devote my life to.

WALLY: Well, I say, "grab all you can!" God helps those who help themselves, right? Hey, I have to go. I have to interview a drummer for the band. So long! *(Exits)*

CARL: Hmmm. He sure wasn't much help. And I'm sure mixed up. *(Exits)*

Scene 4

■

Carl and Pastor Wayne in Pastor Wayne's office

CARL *(Anxious, pacing back and forth)*: Pastor, I'm having a terrible time making decisions. Everyone I talk to has a different idea of how to find God's plan for my life, and I'm so confused I don't know where to start.

WAYNE: Well, I'll sure try to help. But first, you have to calm down! *(Carl stops pacing and moves toward Pastor Wayne and "sits.")* Here, take this Bible *(hands Carl the Bible, or pretends to if your puppets cannot handle the Bible)* and look up Philippians 4:6 (TLB).

CARL *(Looks up the verse.)*: Here it is: "Don't worry about anything; instead, pray about everything; tell God your needs and don't forget to thank him for his answers." That's easy to say, but hard to do.

WAYNE: Have you prayed about these things that are bothering you?

CARL: Well, no. I've been too busy getting advice from all my friends.

WAYNE: Carl, Jesus is the very best Friend you could have. And He wants you to share the things that are bothering you with Him.

CARL *(Hanging his head)*: Yes, I guess you're right.

WAYNE: Let's look up another Scripture. How about Psalm 119:105 (TLB)?

CARL: Okay. Let's see . . . here it is: "Your words are a flashlight to light the path ahead of me, and keep me from stumbling."

WAYNE: What is that verse saying to you?

CARL: Hmmm. Well, I guess it's telling me that God's Word has something to say to me about what my path should be.

WAYNE: That's right.

CARL: But my friends! It seems like every one of them has different advice for me.

WAYNE: Yes, that's going to happen. It's good to seek advice from people who are sensitive to God's presence, God's power, and God's Word whenever possible. But even then, you may get different advice from different people.

CARL: Now you're really confusing me!

WAYNE: My friend, there really aren't any simple formulas for finding God's will. The best thing that I can tell you is to talk to God regularly—get to be a close friend of His—and find what His Word says. And take time to *listen,* too.

CARL: So now what do I do?

WAYNE: Let's just take one day at a time. I'll pray for you every day, and let's meet together once a week. How does that sound?

CARL: It sounds better than any other advice I've had! *(Starts to leave)* Oh, could you write down some of those Bible verses for me? I think I'd like to read some more of them.

WAYNE: Sure! I'd be happy to. I'll give you a list on Sunday.

CARL: Sounds good! *(As he exits)* And. . . thanks for the help!

□

Dale Vonseggen and his wife, Liz, are directors of Puppets from One Way Street and travel thousands of miles each year ministering and doing workshops with puppets. Dale also ministers half time at Denver First Church of the Nazarene, and writes new puppet scripts in his spare time.

Grub and Gab

Photo by Bob Taylor

A ONE-STOP PROGRESSIVE DINNER
For Teens and Adults

Breakaway

Aim

BY MARLENE LEFEVER

To provide a casual atmosphere in which teens and older Christians can interact on the subject of life choices.

Overview

Plan a progressive dinner in one home. Teens and adults will progress from one room to another for each course. With each room change, the people mix at the tables will also change. The dinner helps teens and adults start relationships in a relaxed atmosphere. It also provides an opportunity for kids and adults to discuss their experiences in making life choices, seeking God's will, and striving to live as Christians.

Planning a progressive dinner under one roof has a number of advantages over the more traditional idea where people drive from one house to another:

- You break up traditional groupings of kids. Cliques would tend to travel together. When you mix people under one roof, that won't happen.
- You allow more time for the primary aim of the event—interaction with each other—and take less time traveling.
- You reduce the chance for accidents on the road.
- You give all teens an opportunity to participate equally. Those who can't drive or don't have cars won't be second-class participants.

You'll Need

- ☐ one volunteer home (more if you have a very large group)
- ☐ tables and chairs, enough for three tables of four to six each (more if you need them)
- ☐ three-course meal for a large group (suggested recipes provided)
- ☐ adult guests, same number as student guests
- ☐ adult "servants," one for each table
- ☐ program cards, enough for each guest plus a few extra
- ☐ Progressive Dinner Questions (activity piece BR1 from the back of this book)
- ☐ camera, film, and flash
- ☐ plates, cups, flatware, napkins, and serving utensils

Grub and Gab

One-Stop Progressive Dinner

Soup and salad

Main course

Dessert

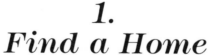

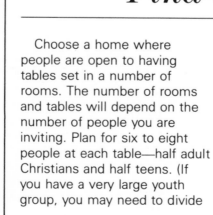

1.
Find a Home

Choose a home where people are open to having tables set in a number of rooms. The number of rooms and tables will depend on the number of people you are inviting. Plan for six to eight people at each table—half adult Christians and half teens. (If you have a very large youth group, you may need to divide it into several smaller groups and find a separate home for each one. Remember that each smaller group should spend the entire evening at the same house.)

Pick an adult to be the "servant" for each table. That person will serve the food, but will not be an active participant in the activities.

Illustration by Donna Nelson

2. Plan the Menu

Keep the meal simple, but you will need to divide it into at least three courses.

Course 1: Soup and salad
Course 2: Main course
Course 3: Dessert

Serve whatever food you would like, but make sure that you have enough to feed a large number of people. Some recipe suggestions for a large group are given at the end of the instructions.

3. Plan Program Cards

You will need to know who is coming to the "Grub and Gab" so you can give each person a card indicating where he or she will sit for each course. A person might change tables or rooms or stay in the same room and have people at the table change. A program card might look like this:

Sarah Johnson
Soup and Salad—Bedroom Table
Main Course—Dining Room Table
Dessert—Small Table in the Living Room

Have a few extra cards ready in case unexpected participants arrive.

People can sit wherever they wish at the assigned table. It will be interesting to see if adults and teens mix more thoroughly as the meal progresses. That would be one visual indication of the evening's success.

Courses should take about a half hour to eat. You need to allow about five minutes between courses for people to find where they are to go next.

4. Prepare Activities

Plan what you want to happen at each table setting. Here are some ideas. Pick those that are most appropriate for your goals.

■ Why not pray after each course? The people at each table would elect someone to thank God for the food that had been eaten and especially for the conversation that took place during the half hour. You might suggest that an adult pray after the first course and teens pray following the next two.

■ You might put questions for discussion under different plates. See "Progressive Dinner Questions" (activity piece

BR1) for some possibilities. Use as many or as few of them as you like. Make up any of your own that you feel are appropriate. Some can be answered by both teens and adults. Others are aimed at adults only. You may want to mark the questions accordingly.

Allow some time which is not filled by programmed questions. Encourage teens and adults to bring their own ideas into the conversation. This means you should have no more than three programmed questions at each setting. More than one person could answer each question.

■ One possible variation of this is to start out with "light" questions during the soup-and-salad course, get down to basics with the main course, and finish up on a funny and friendly note with dessert.

■ Plan for a group picture at each of the tables at each setting. As teens and adults look back on their three pictures, they will recall the evening and perhaps continue to cement relationships.

■ Keep several questions available at all times. These could be carried by the "servants" so if they see conversation isn't working they can throw in a new discussion starter.

■ Have a pair of reporters do an article for the church paper on the evening. One person should be a teen, the other an adult.

Progressive Dinner

Recipe Ideas
Meal designed to serve 24

Soup and Salad

Carol's Corn Chowder
12 large onions, chopped
8 medium potatoes, diced
4 cups chopped celery with leaves
1½ teaspoons salt
12 cups milk
4 cans cream style corn
Cover onions, potatoes, celery with water. Add salt. Cook until tender. Add milk and corn, and reheat. Add salt and pepper to taste.

Herbed Salad
4 heads lettuce, torn
1 package fried bacon (crispy), crumbled
1 dozen hard-boiled eggs, crumbled
Place bacon and egg crumbles over the torn lettuce.

Dressing
2 cups salad oil
4 small onions, sliced
2 cups white vinegar
3 tablespoons mustard
1 cup sugar
3 tablespoons lemon juice
Salad herbs
Mix and add herbs to taste. For example, add 2 tablespoons of oregano or 2 teaspoons of dill weed. Refrigerate four days to allow flavor to penetrate the mixture.

Main Course

Apricot Chicken
6 chickens cut in pieces
3 large jars apricot preserves
3 large jars French dressing
4 packages dried onion soup mix
8 tablespoons Worcestershire sauce
Bake chicken in a buttered, uncovered baking dish for 1 hour at 350°. Mix the rest of the ingredients together, and at the end of the hour, add the sauce to the chicken. Cover tightly and cook 20 minutes longer, or until fork tender.

Rice
4 cups uncooked rice
4 5-ounce cans of water chestnuts, drained and sliced
8 cups hot water
4 tablespoons butter or margarine

Toast rice in a shallow casserole at 350°. Stir occasionally so rice browns evenly. Blend remaining ingredients; stir into rice. Bake covered until rice is tender and liquid is absorbed (about 30 minutes).

Add a vegetable and rolls and butter to this course, if you wish.

Dessert Course

The Raspberry Angel
4 angel food cakes
2 pudding mixes—vanilla is best
1 large jar of raspberry jelly
Carefully slice each cake horizontally to make three layers. Fill the first layer with pudding (Make it according to the directions on the box. Chill thoroughly) and the second with raspberry jelly. Frost with butter frosting.

(Recipes adapted from *Creative Hospitality* by Marlene LeFever. Published by Tyndale House Publishers, Inc. © 1980. Used by permission.)

Marlene LeFever *is a noted Christian educator and youth speaker. She has written several books on creativity, including* Creative Teaching Methods *(Cook, 1985), a large collection of ideas to use with senior high youth.*

DECISION MAKING

Proverbs 3:5, 6
Trust in the Lord with all your heart and lean not on your own understanding; in all your ways acknowledge him, and he will make your paths straight.

Hebrews 11:6
And without faith it is impossible to please God, because anyone who comes to him must believe that he exists and that he rewards those who earnestly seek him.

SEVEN STEPS

FOR DECISION MAKING

1. Pray and ask God for guidance in the whole process.
2. List your values (as they relate to Biblical priorities).
3. Seek counsel from others (if needed).
4. Consider the options (in light of your values).
5. Weigh the consequences of each option (advantages and disadvantages).
6. Make a choice.
7. Take action.

CASE STUDY

Derek is a high school junior and an outstanding athlete. His best sport is baseball, and he believes that if he has a good season this year, he will have a good shot at a college scholarship. Derek wants to go to college, but because of his family financial situation, he knows that he will only be able to go if he gets a scholarship or if he earns enough money. Recently a friend told him about a job opening. It would pay very well and really boost his college savings account. The only trouble is that the job begins during the spring so he would have to quit baseball or only play half a season. What should Derek do?

WARNINGS
WHEN YOU LOOK FOR GOD'S WILL

1 Donkeys & Fleeces

In Numbers 22, God spoke to Balaam through a donkey. And in Judges 6, He used wet and dry fleeces (wool) to affirm His plan to Gideon. The fact is, God can *do anything* and He can *use anything* to communicate His will to us; but don't expect Him to give you a sign to show you what He wants. (For example, "Heal me and I know you want me to be a missionary.") Remember, Jesus told Satan, " 'Do not put the Lord your God to the test' " (Mt. 4:7).

2 Emotions

Emotions can be very persuasive. When you feel good about a decision, you might assume that it is God's choice as well. But emotions are volatile and unreliable. How often a girl is told by more than one guy that it is God's will for her to marry him. . . and him . . . and him . . .?! Obviously at least two of her suitors are misreading what God's will is. Instead, the Bible tells you to renew your mind "that ye may prove what is that good, and acceptable, and perfect, will of God" (Rom. 12:2, KJV). Renewing your mind means making your mind new. It means learning to think about things the way God thinks about them. It means learning to desire and value as God does.

3 American Individualism/ Materialism

In America we are very conscious of the individual. We stress individual freedom and individual rights. This strong emphasis can easily slide into self-centeredness as we look out for number one above everything else. We ask, "What is God's will for *my* life?" Where in Scripture do we find mention of God's will being so individualistic? This is not to say that God is uninterested in the individual; He is! (See Psalm 139.) But instead of focusing our attention on ourselves, we must ask first, "What is God's will for the world and how am I fitting into it?" Jesus taught that the secret to living a day at a time is to "seek ye first the kingdom of God and His righteousness" (Mt. 6:33, KJV).

Closely tied to individualism is materialism. It's a part of our culture—the American dream includes personal ownership and accumulation of possessions. Some Americans believe that God wants all Christians to be wealthy and always healthy. Re-read James 1, however, and you'll find the discussion of God's will immediately following an admonition about facing difficulties and problems. Don't forget that Jesus was crucified and that millions have suffered and died for their faith. (In John 16:33, Jesus warned the disciples that they would have trouble in the world.) Clearly God's will may be to take at least some of us through some pretty rough times.

4 Limited Perspective

Perspective is a point of view, a way of seeing things. As finite human beings, our perspective is severely limited. Your three-year-old brother, for example, may think he knows everything . . . but you know better. His perspective is limited by his age and experience. Or look at a picture about an inch away from your eyes— you will see a blur of colors or dots. As you move it away, the picture begins to come into focus. Your original perspective was limited because of your closeness to the picture.

In contrast, God's perspective is unlimited. He's seen it all and He sees it all. God sees the whole picture. He knows about events, circumstances, and people totally outside your line of vision. Proverbs 3:5, 6 promises that God will direct your paths. If there's a secret, it's to trust and acknowledge Him in all your ways and to "lean not" (put all your weight) "on your own understanding."

D E T E R M I N I N G

GOD'S WILL

Look up your assigned passage(s) and answer these questions:

- What does the verse say?
- How does it apply to decision making?

1. Matthew 6:33, 34

2. Luke 16:10

3. Philippians 4:6

4. II Timothy 2:15; 3:16, 17

5. Proverbs 20:5, 18

6. Romans 12:2; James 1:5

7. Luke 9:62; James 1:6-8

Create-a-Date

What's your dream date like? If you're not satisfied with what life's offered you so far, why don't you create your own? Just choose the characteristics you like best and put them together to see how they match. Watch out, you may learn something in the process.

This *material girl* could run you wild.

Watch out that he doesn't treat you like he treats his guitar.

The horsey set. Old money.

Beware that Ultra-Brite® smile!

He sure can pass the football, but he's not too sure about English.

She's the bubbly type.

He's got all the lines, but is it just for show?

Shy, but a good friend.

Kind of a nerd, but sweet.

This guy's really got his head in the clouds.

Bookworm.

Illustration by Craig Yoe

Advertise Yourself

The following personals are based on actual ads placed in the *New York Review*.

Nice-looking, available man. Artist-writer-professor. Seeks leading lady for collaboration on life script. Bright, perceptive, thoughtful, and unusually sensitive. Generally considered a little shy with women. Seeking affectionate, intelligent, reasonably well-figured woman, with understated good looks, self-confident but not too narcissistic, who might appreciate my good qualities, overlook my flaws, and work with me toward a lasting partnership.

Beautiful, loyal, outdoorsy "collie" lady would like to meet faithful, domesticated, midwestern "St. Bernard" gentleman.

Want a real man, lady? Loving conversation exhilarates me. Tenderness brings happy tears. Warm, sexy women devastate me. Authentic Man.

Sense of humor essential! I'm attractive, love museums, bicycling, good music, a good laugh. Would like to meet attractive man with integrity who is as uncomfortable about this as I am.

Man seeks woman.

Consult God's standards for character in I Peter 3:3, 4; I Thessalonians 4:3-8; and Galatians 5:13-26 and write your own personal ad.

Who, Me?

1. Yes, you! As in the parable, God has given all of us gifts to use in His service. List below all the skills, abilities, talents, resources, or anything else you can think of, that you have been given. Try to run out of room—this is no time to be modest!

_____

_____

_____

_____

_____

_____

_____

2. Listed below are 15 attributes that prospective employers often look for in job candidates. Rank them from one to fifteen in terms of how important you think each one is. After you're done, you'll find out how actual employers ranked them.

Attribute	Your Ranking	Their Ranking
Appearance	☐	☐
Assertiveness	☐	☐
Disposition	☐	☐
Enthusiasm	☐	☐
Extroversion	☐	☐
Grades	☐	☐
Initiative	☐	☐
Leadership	☐	☐
Loyalty	☐	☐
Maturity	☐	☐
Motivation	☐	☐
Oral communication	☐	☐
Punctuality	☐	☐
Work experience	☐	☐
Written communication	☐	☐

3. Some Advice:

1. Work your hardest at whatever job you have, no matter how difficult or boring it is. Skills you develop now will stay with you the rest of your life.

2. Look for jobs in the future that develop your areas of interest. If you like people, you'd be better off as a waiter or waitress than as a dishwasher.

3. Look for jobs that take advantage of your skills. If you're an athlete, maybe there's work as a clerk at a sporting goods store.

4. Look for jobs that fit your values. If you value being slim, think twice before working at the local ice-cream parlor!

5. Talk to your school counselor about future schooling/jobs.

What Do You Want Out of Life?

Please complete these statements honestly:

1. I wish I had . . .
   these additional possessions: _____

   _____

   this additional amount of money: $ _____   (use back of sheet if necessary)

2. I believe having money will make you:
   _____secure   _____desired as a friend   _____happy
   _____insecure   _____unhappy
   _____worried   _____comfortable   _____a potential kidnap victim

3. I would define "having enough money" as having enough to enable me to:_____

4. Possessions make a person happy when:_____

5. Possessions make a person unhappy when:_____

ACTIVITY PIECE E1 by Sandy Larsen © 1986 David C. Cook Publishing Co. Permission granted to reproduce for ministry use only—not for resale.

What's Money For?

(Some Biblical Ideas)

Read Ecclesiastes 5:10-20 and locate the *opposite* of the following statements. In the blank, write the verse number(s) and then a summary of what the Bible *actually* says.

1. The wealthier you are on earth, the wealthier you will be in Heaven.

2. If God gives you lots of material things, be careful to keep a sour face and not enjoy them too much.

3. Once you've reached your financial goals, you will finally be satisfied.

4. Money guarantees emotional security.

5. Owning a lot is a guarantee that you'll have something to leave your children.

6. Work is slavery and drudgery and not worth the effort.

NOW ANSWER THIS:
What general conclusions can you draw from Ecclesiastes 5:10-20?

Money/possessions can give you:

Money/possessions cannot give you:

ACTIVITY PIECE E2 by Sandy Larsen © 1986 David C. Cook Publishing Co. Permission granted to reproduce for ministry use only—not for resale.

PROGRESSIVE DINNER
Q U E S T I O N S

SOUP AND SALAD
What are some of the life choices you have made? Which were most difficult?

SOUP AND SALAD
How does being a Christian affect your life choices?

SOUP AND SALAD
What's the most difficult goal you set for yourself and reached?

SOUP AND SALAD
How did you know what you wanted to do for a living?

SOUP AND SALAD
How did you prepare for your job? What do you wish you had done differently?

SOUP AND SALAD
How does a person know it's the right time to get married? Why do so many people make mistakes?

SOUP AND SALAD
I've heard a lot about mid-life crisis. Have you had one? What is it like?

SOUP AND SALAD
How do you decide how to spend your money? How does being a Christian play a part?

MAIN COURSE
How do you handle disappointments when things honestly don't turn out the way you want them to?

MAIN COURSE
As a teen (adult), what advice do you have to give on making successful choices?

MAIN COURSE
People talk a lot about the Lord leading them. How do you know He does, based on your personal experience?

MAIN COURSE
Why do some of our best laid plans fail?

MAIN COURSE
If you had a million dollars given to you, what would you do with it? What if you had to spend it all in one year?

MAIN COURSE
What is the hardest thing you've faced in your marriage? What did you think would be the hardest before you got married?

MAIN COURSE
What's a choice you made that you wish you hadn't?

DESSERT
On the job, what do you struggle most with?

DESSERT
How important is money to you?

DESSERT
What's one goal you have for your life that you would like to reach in the next five years?

DESSERT
Next to becoming a Christian, what's been your biggest life choice?

DESSERT
How do you go about making difficult decisions?